Praise for *Serial Fixer*

"You are your tool: More than a mantra, it's a truism. For all of us serving individuals, teams, and organizations, this is critical to live into. And if true, one must take care of the tool to be of any use to others. Leah Marone serves all of us well in bringing the insight of a therapist, the strategy of a coach, and the wisdom of a mentor to all of us seeking to know how to care for ourselves as we serve others. If you are on the journey of moving from serial fixer to healthy guide, you must read this book!"

—**Kurt André**, CEO of Transformational Coaching and Consulting International and cofounder of the Consulting Academy

"Leah Marone's *Serial Fixer* is a compassionate and deeply insightful guide for those trapped in the exhausting cycle of solving other people's problems. With sharp psychological wisdom and practical tools, Marone helps readers break codependent patterns and nurture healthier, more authentic relationships. Whether you struggle with boundaries, people-pleasing, or emotional burnout, this book offers the understanding and strategies needed to support others without losing yourself in the process. A must-read for reclaiming your emotional well-being."

—**Jessica Baum**, LMHC, author of *Anxiously Attached: Becoming More Secure in Life and Love*

"Sometimes it feels like we're all just struggling to stay afloat. If you're more worried about the other occupants of your life raft than yourself, it might be time to scoop up *Serial Fixer*. It will be your lifeline."

—**Bobbie Carlton**, founder of Innovation Women

"As an educator and serial fixer, I was drowning in my school's endless needs. Marone's transformative book taught me to create essential boundaries without compromising my authentic self. I've learned to support others without becoming overwhelmed by their challenges. This powerful resource provides practical frameworks for educators to maintain presence and connection while protecting their well-being—a must-read for anyone who gives deeply but struggles to save space for themselves."

—**Leah Carper**, 2022 North Carolina
Teacher of the Year

"Leah Marone has written a must-read for every selfless caregiver who often loses themselves in others' needs. She shows high achievers that caring for others doesn't have to mean neglecting yourself. I'll be recommending *Serial Fixer* to my clients who strive to be everything for everyone except themselves."

—**Dr. Therese Mascardo**, psychologist and
author of *Love the Journey*

"So many high performers are quietly unraveling behind polished exteriors, desperate to feel like enough. *Serial Fixer* exposes the stories we tell ourselves to earn worth through constant doing—and then gently guides us back to the truth of who we are. This book is a powerful companion for anyone recovering from the belief that their value is tied to their usefulness."

—**Lisa McGuire**, EdS, business growth and reinvention
strategist, host of the *Your Passion, Purpose
and Personal Brand* podcast

"If you're seeking emotional intelligence that deepens relational awareness and promotes purposeful problem-solving—without getting stuck fixing others or avoiding your own reflection—then check out *Serial Fixer* by Leah Marone. As a leading psychotherapist, Marone masterfully delivers a guide that helps improve your relationships with others and yourself. *Serial Fixer* is a must-read, a riveting book that reframes the art of problem-solving. This book will leave you longing for more and will help you break free from the habit of solving other people's problems."

—**Manny Ohonme**, cofounder, president, and CEO of Samaritan's Feet International

"*Serial Fixer* offers valuable tools for setting boundaries, living mindfully, and overcoming unhealthy habits. This book stands out by helping readers recognize their patterns by observing how a psychotherapist, Leah Marone, works with serial fixers. The book is divided into three parts, each offering valuable strategies: Part 1 examines the traits of a serial fixer and patterns that keep them trapped in their urge to fix others. Part 2 focuses on boundaries, self-trust, and how to create space between yourself and others. Part 3 highlights the importance of validating, empathizing, and offering support without attempting to solve others' problems. If you're struggling with the urge to fix, this book is for you."

—**Barbara Rubel**, MA, BCETS, DAAETS, author of *But I Didn't Say Goodbye* and *Living Blue*

SERIAL FIXER

SERIAL FIXER

Break Free from the Habit of Solving Other People's Problems

LEAH MARONE

Broadleaf Books
Minneapolis

SERIAL FIXER
Break Free from the Habit of Solving Other People's Problems

31 30 29 28 27 26 25 1 2 3 4 5 6 7 8 9

To protect the privacy of individuals, names, characteristics, and identifying details have been changed. Some events have been modified or fictionalized for illustrative purposes.

Library of Congress Control Number: 2025003316 (print)

Cover design by Broadleaf Books
Cover image: © 2025 Getty Images; Hand/97235468 by CSA Images

Print ISBN: 979-8-8898-3533-2
eBook ISBN: 979-8-8898-3534-9

Printed in India.

To all of the fixers. The selflessly intended leaders and caretakers. Those who give deeply, sometimes losing touch with themselves along the way.

Contents

Introduction

5:30 a.m.: Your alarm goes off. You had every intention of starting your workout routine today—it's Monday, the unofficial day of fresh starts. But exhaustion weighs on you, a consequence of being up between 2:00 and 3:30 a.m., replaying your brother's cryptic text in your head: "I'm done with my marriage and everything in-between. What's the point?" You offered calming words, but he didn't respond. You can't shake the worry.

6:00 a.m.: You grab your phone, guilt nudging you out of bed. A text from your neighbor asks for help taking her kids to school again. Saying no feels impossible, so you reply with a thumbs-up emoji, determined to make it work even though asking your partner for help doesn't feel like an option. Notifications flood in, pulling you into the day before you've even had a moment to breathe.

7:00 a.m.: Your phone buzzes again—it's a text from your coworker. She needs help with a project. Without thinking, you rearrange your morning to assist, prioritizing her needs over your own.

12:00 p.m.: Lunchtime arrives, but it's not much of a break. You scarf down a half sandwich while juggling work, your mind racing through a growing list of responsibilities, and you scroll social media.

3:00 p.m.: At your desk, your phone buzzes again: Your brother has finally texted back, but his message only leaves you more worried. The day is slipping away. You're scattered, thinking about unfinished work, an email you forgot to send, and the meeting starting soon.

5:00 p.m.: As you're getting ready to leave, you touch base with your coworker. She's still stressed and needs you. You offer to stay late and help, pushing your own plans aside once more. Maybe you should ask your partner to pick up the slack at home, even though you promised to be there—but that might be too much for them. You try to figure out what can be delivered to the house for dinner as you make a mad dash for the parking garage.

7:30 p.m.: Finally home, you try to be present with your family, though your energy is drained. You realize you never followed up with your brother. Your mind flips through the wins you secured for others today—your neighbor, your coworker—while your own needs were delayed again. The kitchen feels quiet for a moment, but soon your teenager marches in, huffing about her homework and annoyance with school. Before you've even set down your bag, you start offering solutions: "Maybe you need to start earlier. Have you tried making a schedule? I will email your teacher again." Your words tumble out, dismissing the raw vulnerability in her voice. She rolls her eyes, muttering, "You don't get it." You pour a glass of wine, searching for a moment of relief even though you know it'll make the sleepless hours of the night more difficult. As the day ends, that familiar feeling returns: Despite everything, you still didn't do enough.

And the cycle continues as the next day begins.

Fixing isn't the same as helping. In fact, it's likely causing more harm—to others, to yourself, and to the very connections you value most. While stepping in to solve someone else's problems might feel satisfying in the moment, it comes at a cost.

Sure, fixing may bring you temporary relief. It validates your sense of purpose and lets you skip the patience required for genuine listening. Many of us like to think we're great listeners, but are we really? Fixing robs others of the chance to face their challenges, build resilience, and gain the confidence that comes from navigating difficulties on their own. Instead, it provides immediate closure—a problem checked off your list, feeding into the relentless rhythm of productivity. Ah the list, the ultimate emblem of efficiency. While it can keep us organized and driven, it often narrows our perspective so much that we miss the chance to be truly present and create meaningful space for ourselves and those we care about.

I've seen this cycle unfold countless times and lived it myself: compassionate people who struggle to set boundaries. They're constantly checking in on others and encouraging self-care yet fail to show that same grace to themselves. The imbalance is pervasive but easily overlooked. Worse, many never stop to examine the deeper patterns keeping them trapped in these roles—the internal drivers that compel them to repeat behaviors that lead to familiar emotional exhaustion.

The fallout is everywhere. I've witnessed nonprofits closing their doors, corporate teams losing their brightest members to burnout, teachers losing their passion, caregivers collapsing under relentless pressure, friends sacrificing themselves to enable others, and families breaking apart under the weight of unmet needs and unspoken boundaries. Time and again, the lack of clear boundaries doesn't just strain relationships: It erodes them completely, robbing people of the very connection they're striving so hard to preserve.

This book is for the "serial fixer," someone who has great intentions when it comes to helping others but is exhausted and doesn't seem to be getting the desired results or fulfilling connections with others. Whether you are someone that aims to guide, lead, or support one person or a thousand—this book is for you. Perhaps you've been feeling like situations in your life shouldn't be as difficult or draining as they are. Maybe you have acquired unwanted resentment that is slowly engulfing your ability to connect with or lead others. You may have trouble creating or maintaining healthy boundaries that honor who you are and who you aim to be. You might feel taken advantage of at times, but you do not take any steps to set boundaries or change the dynamic of your relationships. Or perhaps you aim to please and would go to extreme lengths to avoid negative associations, conflicts, or judgments. Does this sound like you yet?

This isn't just another self-help book; it's a guide to becoming a mindful and impactful friend, leader, parent, or professional. It's about dismantling the urgency that plagues our modern lives and rediscovering the beauty in presence, authenticity, and sustainable connections. This is a relational reframe helping you play roles that aim to empower and support other people without the consequences and **burnout** occurring from the unnecessary pressure to fix, solve, and control. Join this transformative journey and reclaim your role as a beacon of support without sacrificing your own well-being.

burnout—A state of extreme exhaustion and reduced interest due to prolonged overwork and lack of recovery time. Burnout typically arises when personal boundaries are weak or demands are unrelenting.

Once people learn that I am a psychotherapist and mental wellness consultant, they tend to ask one of two questions: "Are you psychoanalyzing me right now?" and "How do you do what you do without it impacting your well-being?" The first question is typically asked with a nervous grin or a forced chuckle. I attempt to soothe those nerves and add a bit of humor: "Nope, I am not on the clock." Comprehensively analyzing everyone in my daily path would leave me utterly exhausted and suffocate my ability to "just be" and experience life through a balanced lens—one that includes me.

As to the second question, I do indeed have a tendency to allow others' **emotions**, needs, and wants to dictate my own. I am often labeled as carefree or laid-back. Right or wrong, I'm not rocked when plans don't go as expected, nor do I have strong opinions about the details or agenda. This quality comes in very handy, but it also overshadows opportunities for self-reflection and advocating for myself. My inner monologue used to replay these narratives:

> **emotions**—Responses to interactions, decisions, or thoughts, reflecting both conscious and unconscious interpretations of experiences.

I will adjust.
I will accommodate.
I will endure and be fine.
I will continue to avoid this conflict.

This approach has allowed me to enter new chapters of life with minimal external expectations. While the expectations I hold for myself are fiercely high and sometimes self-sabotaging, the expectations I set for others are far less demanding. However, this imbalance leads to feelings of resentment and disconnect, leaving me in situations where immediate, intense boundaries were required—boundaries that should have been established from the start but were avoided.

Since I was young, I've been fascinated by others' stories, experiences, and emotions. I cried at almost every drama movie I saw (let's be honest, still do) and was drawn to classmates who had different cultural norms or backgrounds from my own. I found it fascinating to learn how various perspectives could shape experiences; each exchange was an opportunity to learn something new. When a friend or peer shared with me information in confidence, just me, I felt special and needed. I was intrigued. In my mind, I saw this as an invitation—one that required me to create space, show empathy, or help them through a hurdle.

My curiosity about others' stories and experiences persisted with age. My goal as a clinician has always been to create a safe environment and empower others to depend on themselves, not me. I want to orchestrate and build opportunities that exude vulnerability and foster authentic connection—moments that challenge my clients to do the hard work and celebrate their wins. Therapy is powerful because it encourages true presence. I am consistently humbled and honored to be part of this intimate experience that creates safety and builds trust.

As the therapist, I am not in the spotlight. I am not really even onstage. I have the privilege of being a facilitator of personal growth, but I am not required or expected to share or be vulnerable myself. In the beginning, I didn't prioritize taking care of my own emotional needs, and like many serial fixers, I ultimately paid the price, constantly grappling with emotional hangovers as I stepped in and out of the spotlight, and on and off the stage. I felt the weight of each session as I carried my clients' pain with me, even outside of the therapy room. Over time, I became exhausted, less present, and struggled to separate my clients' struggles from my own. It was as if I was losing myself in the process.

Meet Sofia

Sofia and I had been working together for a few months. As a serial fixer, one of her strengths was her ability to access and share her emotions in therapy. Yet in her everyday life, she often shoved those feelings aside, burying them beneath her drive to support others. She always came into each session with a plan and a sense of direction, and I could clearly see the heavy load she bore when she entered my office. Within the first few minutes, she slowly shed her mental burdens as she externally processed and connected with her thoughts and feelings. Like many, Sofia used therapy as a space to declutter.

She was primed for therapy, ready to open up and activate the skills and reframing techniques she had learned already throughout life's journey. She was in a chapter of her life that allowed her to connect with herself in a new way—open-minded and ready for change. Others had already played important roles with Sofia by planting valuable seeds of wisdom and support, and I was in the unique position of watching her "bloom" and become a new version of herself. As I realized I had the opportunity to help her unravel and apply all the goodness and support she had received over the years, I felt immense gratitude toward those unnamed and influential faces from her past who weren't there to see it all come together.

As coaches, leaders, educators, clinicians, parents, and mentors, we know how rare and special it is when you get the privilege of watching someone bloom. More often than not, we get to plant the seeds and build trust, but the magic of self-discovery and growth unfold later, away from what we get to see and experience. With Sofia, I had the honor of being part of her transformation, watching her connection with herself take flight in new ways that I know we will both remember.

As one of our sessions came to an end, I watched Sofia slowly shrug her shoulders and take a deep breath, almost as if she was letting go of the mental clutter that she brought with her just fifty-five minutes ago. She paused and said, "I feel like I just 'word vomited' all over your office. I talk for the majority of the time, but what you ask and how you respond to me organize my thoughts and feelings. It's almost as if you're a sculptor, carefully chipping away at certain parts of me to reveal what fits and smoothing out the pieces that don't align." That, to date, is one of the best visuals of therapy that a client has given me and continues to make this work so extraordinary.

Therapy is different from most other relationships. It is meant to be imbalanced. My role is to create a space that is conducive for clarity, processing feelings, and guiding people to make connections to improve wellness and intrinsic connection. Building this skill isn't only valuable in my work with clients but has also benefitted me in all types of relationships outside of my office. My personal and professional relationships may have different goals and intimacy levels, but providing space for others and allowing them to explore and maintain ownership of their journey prevents **compassion fatigue** and limits the effects that **vicarious trauma** can have on empathic individuals.

> **compassion fatigue**—A state of emotional and physical exhaustion that arises from prolonged exposure to the suffering or needs of others without sufficient personal recovery time. It often leads to feelings of detachment and reduced empathy, mood, and motivation.
>
> **vicarious trauma**—The emotional impact and fatigue that results from being repeatedly exposed to others' suffering and intense experiences.

Throughout my education and professional experiences, two significant lessons emerged: "Do no harm" and "It's not about you." I learned to avoid self-disclosure in sessions and in relating to clients' personal issues, a topic that has sparked debate in recent years but remains a fundamental truism. Regardless of the client's current state or mindset, my goal is to dedicate our time for them to be heard, seen, and understood. This framework or objective holds true for various roles involving leading, coaching, or mentoring. It's not a space to alleviate my insecurities by sharing personal experiences and seeking accolades or attention. Recognizing that it's not about me as the therapist, if I ever felt the inclination to relate or share a personal story, I knew to address it elsewhere with someone else, keeping in mind the defined role and objective that "it's not about me." As we explore the concepts in this book, including the "Support, Don't Solve" framework, we'll examine how the serial fixer can foster the genuine connections they value while also protecting their own mental health. We'll move beyond the familiar **self-care** lists and well-known analogies like "you have to take care of yourself before you can take care of others." Building resilience and self-connection requires a commitment to deeply understanding your patterns, motivations, and behaviors—without solely relying on pacifiers and Band-Aids.

self-care—Consistent actions to nurture one's emotional, spiritual, physical, and relational well-being. Self-care includes regular self-check-ins and engaging in practices that help maintain proactive, healthy living.

Part 1

The Serial Fixer

If I had to take a guess, curiosity played a large part in your decision to open this book. You likely asked yourself, "What is a serial fixer, and would I be considered one?" If this resonates with you or reminds you of someone you know, read on.

A serial fixer is driven by compassion and a deep desire to connect. Yet somewhere along the way, this well-intended instinct can backfire. While it feels productive to step in, solve problems, and immediately smooth things over, it often comes at a cost not just to you but also to the people you lead and care about.

In the first part of this book, we'll explore the inner workings of the serial fixer: the drivers, internal conflicts, and hidden patterns that keep them stuck in the relentless urge to fix. You'll learn how certain behavior cycles and loose boundaries take an emotional toll and foster dependencies in relationships. The efforts made to achieve genuine connection and purpose shouldn't result in resentment or create spaces where symptoms of burnout can quietly creep in.

Are you ready? Let's dive in.

Chapter 1

Are You a "Serial Fixer"?

The Serial Fixer

The privilege that comes with being a psychotherapist is one that's hard to replicate in other professions. You gather data in a way that's raw, unpredictable, and insightful about the inner workings of human beings. I've noticed a common thread, whether I'm working with a client or connecting with a friend: So many of us feel overwhelmed by life and unfulfilled in relationships. We are confused why it seems so hard to access what we crave most: true, authentic connections. While we can certainly place some of the blame on societal changes, including the fact that we increasingly communicate through devices, we must also look inside ourselves. Our relentless drive to control and fix things—often as a way to protect ourselves—can lead to self-sabotage. Maybe our efforts are being directed toward the wrong places. Perhaps we're unaware or out of sync with the inner drivers and barriers that should lead to fulfilling connections. The problem for most of us is that we lack a true connection with ourselves. What we're truly missing is the **self-awareness** needed to begin and sustain this kind of inner work.

> **self-awareness**—An ongoing process of recognizing and understanding one's thoughts, emotions, and behaviors in real time. Self-awareness includes noticing shifts in one's energy or mood and using this information to set boundaries or make adjustments as needed.

As you venture further into this book, you may feel a mix of curiosity and uncertainty. Books that explore deep-seated traits and patterns can stir a range of emotions. Some parts of you might be eager to connect with the ideas ahead, while others may feel more guarded or skeptical. You might even find yourself somewhere in between, unsure of what to expect. But keep an open mind. Take your time, take notes, and allow this book to be an opportunity to explore and align with the internal responses that arise as you dive deeper.

I was trained to recognize and highlight the strengths behind a person's actions. But let's be real—as a recovering serial fixer, this instinct was automatic, even excessive, long before it became a honed skill. The problem was that I aimed to help and soothe everyone else without taking the time necessary for myself. Serial fixers possess admirable qualities—attributes that foster connection, positivity, and care. However, the challenge we'll explore is how these actions, when taken to excess, can create detrimental imbalances and impact our own well-being and relationships. Compassion flows outward but is rarely allowed back in. Serial fixers are exceptional givers yet often struggle with the vulnerability of receiving or letting others care for them. They also find it hard to create the same nurturing spaces for themselves and feel confused when relationships seem one-sided or when their efforts go unreciprocated. If any of that sounds familiar to you, I'd encourage you to take a breath, open your mind, and remind yourself that by choosing to do something for you, you've already made an important step forward.

The word *serial* refers to an action or event that repeatedly occurs, suggesting an identifiable pattern. A *serial fixer*, then, is someone who frequently places themselves in the role of fixer or solver of problems that are not their own. They typically possess a high level of emotional intelligence and have an intense desire to help others. In addition, this drive aligns with their ego, continually affirming their sense of purpose, their ability to understand others and others' nuances, and their capacity for problem-solving. Individuals attracted to professions requiring high compassion and the ability to sift through emotional situations very often wind up using the struggles of others as a means to structure their own lives. This tendency confirms their sense of purpose and connection. However, they rarely provide themselves with the same courtesy, care, and space. Helping others by immersing themselves into the layers of others' challenges presents itself as easier and more rewarding compared to navigating their own issues. The majority of their emotional and problem-solving energy is allocated to other people, leaving very little room for self-connection and recovery.

The motto of a typical serial fixer might sound like this: "As long as I'm helping, I have purpose—and therefore, I can endure." Often, helping others and focusing on external issues provides structure that feels easier than looking inward to break our own cycles. This allows the serial fixer to avoid, often justifiably, giving themselves the care they need to build self-connection, adopt healthier mindsets, or address the parts of themselves that are quietly, but persistently, demanding attention.

The serial fixer is a good listener but quickly assumes the role of problem solver. In some interactions, they leave feeling energized and unburdened; it's fulfilling. The conversation was productive, and they walk away feeling heard and useful. The space they created benefited someone, reaffirming their competence and helpfulness, and all seems well. Their ego is content and craves to replicate this cycle. Though they continue to create space for others, they often take on most of the problem-solving or emotional labor.

This dynamic sets the stage for relationships to become perpetually imbalanced and, at times, fosters dependence. In these situations, one person consistently assumes the role of caregiver or fixer, while the other depends on them for emotional support or solutions. It's important to note that balanced relationships don't always mean a fifty-fifty split—sometimes one person carries more of the load, and that's okay. The key is that in healthy relationships, this ebb and flow happens naturally. In **imbalanced relationships**, the roles become fixed, leaving one person overburdened. The fixer carves out a definitive, yet enabling role that inevitably leads to frustration, exhaustion, or resentment. Boundaries are loose or nonexistent, and the daunting task of setting them later is often avoided out of fear of others' reactions. Serial fixers are always available: as leaders, they subscribe to the open-door policy; as parents, they are the planners, organizers, and solvers; as friends, they're constantly there to hash out and solve others' problems, even in the middle of the night—often leaving themselves exhausted and drained the next day.

> **imbalanced relationships**—Relationships where one person is always giving more support, effort, and structure than the other. This can lead to one person feeling taken advantage of. While all relationships have ups and downs, an imbalanced relationship is consistently one-sided, with one person doing most of the work.

You Might Be a Serial Fixer If You

- Tend to feel "heavier" or overwhelmed after conversations with others.
- Place yourself in the role of the fixer or solver in relationships.
- Take pride in helping others open up and be vulnerable, but you struggle to do the same for yourself.

- Have a way of convincing yourself that "you're good" if everyone around you is.
- Neglect your own needs and well-being often to attend to others' problems.
- Feel a sense of guilt or **anxiety** if you are not able to help someone.
- Find it difficult to say no to people who need help, even when you are overwhelmed.
- Feel responsible for the emotions and outcomes of others' lives.
- Struggle with setting boundaries and often overextend yourself.

anxiety—Persistent worry or fear that often prevents you from living in the present. Anxiety can involve excessive dwelling on the past (rumination) or overpreparing for the future, leading to intense physical and emotional responses. It stems from internal mental processes and can interfere with confidence, presence, and clear thinking.

- Derive your sense of self-worth from being needed or useful to others.
- Feel often unappreciated or taken for granted in your relationships.
- Tend to attract people who are dependent or who rely heavily on your support.
- Have a pattern of getting involved in others' conflicts, trying to mediate or resolve issues.
- Feel restless or anxious when you are not helping or doing something for someone.
- Find yourself often fixing the same problems repeatedly for the same people.
- Believe that if you don't intervene, things will fall apart or people will fail.
- Have a hard time accepting help or support from others.
- Are always available.

Serial fixers thrive in environments where organization, scheduling, and structuring are essential. In some relationships, this meticulous attention to detail is not only appreciated but necessary, although it may not always be recognized or validated. Fixers often go above and beyond in their roles, driven by a deep-seated need to control and take charge of another person's care, which becomes a significant part of their identity and purpose. This dynamic leads to imbalance in relationships, where someone either takes advantage of the serial fixer's efforts or feels compelled to set a **boundary**, leaving the serial fixer feeling confused, resentful, or abandoned.

boundary—A personal limit set to protect a person's comfort, health, or energy, often based on past experiences or personal needs. Boundaries may be physical, emotional, or temporal.

Types of Serial Fixers

Saints

The first type of serial fixer is the "saint," who always prioritizes others. They have been conditioned to maintain their smile and live each day to its most positive version, which is beautiful and effective—when they include themselves too. However, like anything else, awareness is key. Recognizing and addressing one's own emotions that may be labeled as negative is difficult but essential. Saints are either out of practice or have become incredibly adept at hiding these emotions, such that they frequently encounter symptoms of anxiety and depression. Nonetheless, their "good fight" continues as they push forward, relying on suppression as a coping mechanism.

Saints are highly attuned to the needs and emotional shifts of others and use this emotional knowledge to determine how they will proceed, react, or respond. Saints ignore that perhaps they didn't sleep yet again due to antagonizing thoughts or pangs of self-doubt because they didn't stick to a personal goal set months ago. They tell themselves, "People need me," and their needs can once again be put on hold. "I can't be selfish. I have to be there for my friends and family. This is what I do. It's my purpose." Saints fear what they might be left with—or not left with—if they abandon their role as a fixer. The unfamiliar space, a space meant for just them, is scary and not a reality they're equipped to navigate or structure.

Doormats

The second type of serial fixer takes on the role of "doormat." Doormats are vulnerable to being taken advantage of by others. This is not usually due to malicious intent on the part of those around them; rather, doormats consistently place themselves in this position by being excessively available and overaccommodating. While boundaries are essential for others, and they may help others establish or maintain those boundaries, they often don't replicate this process for themselves. They take on more than their fair share of responsibilities, often feeling like the glue that holds everything together, believing that if they stop, everything will fall apart.

Concerns about how others might perceive them or react have outsized levels of importance with doormats. An overwhelming fear of abandonment or rejection drives their behavior. They adhere to mottos like "avoid confrontation at all costs," even when a minor conflict would significantly benefit their well-being. This fear prevents them from saying no or advocating for their perspective and preferences, reinforcing a cycle of self-neglect. Beneath the surface, however, resentment steadily builds in doormats. Doormats typically develop strong feelings of resentment when they see their contributions to others go unnoticed or they fail to receive the same reciprocated acts of care and kindness. Despite the strength of these feelings, they struggle to voice them openly. Instead, their frustrations are often expressed through passive-aggressive behaviors or indirect communication, which confuses those around them and erodes relationships.

A doormat's reluctance to assert themselves, combined with an overreliance on external validation, leaves them emotionally and physically drained. They rarely ask for help themselves, fearing they will be seen as burdensome. In some cases, this behavior stems from chaotic family dynamics when they were young and takes time and patience to explore and address. Doormats were often made responsible for soothing or stabilizing situations they weren't old enough to handle, compensating for adults who struggled with emotional regulation and structure. These environments and relationships cultivated the doormat's sense of obligation while neglecting their ability to care for and trust themselves.

Over time, doormats become so focused on meeting the needs of others that they lose sight of their own identity and desires. This neglect of the self stunts personal and professional growth, depriving doormats of practice in asserting their needs and boundaries. They feel unfulfilled in their relationships, absorbing unhealthy amounts of responsibility without ever feeling truly seen or valued. Two outcomes can occur as a result of this behavior: Others take advantage of them, as doormats often appear willing to please and accommodate without asking anything in return; conversely, some hesitate to rely on or collaborate with them, sensing their uncertainty and lack of self-assurance. They may doubt whether the doormat will express genuine thoughts or simply conform to others' needs until they reach a breaking point.

Steamrollers

The last group of serial fixers, the "steamrollers," are rigid in their approach. They leave little room for deviation from their plan or anything that disrupts the predictable sequence they believe is best. Quick to solve and fix, they rush to check things off their to-do list, striving for peace, stability, and calm. However, their game is infinite, because they're always on to the next task, chasing a sense of control that remains ever out of reach.

Rigidity defines their approach. While the idea of being open-minded may sound appealing, it's far from their natural practice. They pride themselves on being knowledgeable, but they approach conversations with an aggressive need to teach what they know. With this craving to explain, they leave little room to assess how others might feel or where they are in the process. Steamrollers are unconcerned with these details and push forward, rattling off their opinions and instructions with little regard for others' input. They expect others to follow their exact, explained path and hope to be affirmed for their efforts, craving acknowledgment that reinforces their sense of competence, expertise, or control.

Steamrollers frequently interrupt, operating with a one-track mind and leaving no space for collaboration. Conversations become one-sided, more of a lecture than an exchange, leaving others wondering if they were truly heard. Their rigid, impatient, and protective approach shields them from engaging with ideas that could bring discomfort or emotional challenges. Fear of discomfort drives them, and they avoid it at all costs.

As a result, they absorb unhealthy and unrealistic amounts of responsibility, often unclear about what is truly theirs to own, so they take it all on. Steamrollers struggle to trust others, believing that if they don't do everything, nothing will be done properly. Ironically, their approach makes collaboration difficult, causing others to hesitate when it comes to engaging with or challenging them. Their dismissive or controlling responses signal to colleagues and friends that it's "my way or the highway." This leaves others reluctant to communicate or collaborate.

This avoidance of emotion-driven situations stunts their growth in all kinds of relationships. In friendships, they play the role of the know-it-all, dominating conversations and leaving little room for emotional exchange. Professionally, they stagnate, lacking the leadership skills necessary to foster empathetic, emotionally intelligent, and curious cultures. These skills remain underdeveloped because they don't practice them. As a result, steamrollers often find themselves stuck, unsure why their approach isn't yielding the fulfillment or team engagement they seek.

Deep levels of connection and intimacy are difficult for them to achieve. Steamrollers excel at fixing processes and tangible tasks, but they recoil when unfamiliar emotions arise, leaving them feeling lost and unsure how to proceed. This stagnation, both in personal relationships and at work, stems from their inability to engage with the softer skills—empathy and curiosity—that are essential for leading healthy, balanced teams and relationships.

At the core of all serial fixers is a tendency to overextend themselves for others, often at the expense of their own well-being. Whether it's the saints' relentless focus on maintaining a positive image, the doormat's excessive accommodation and people-pleasing behaviors, or the steamroller's rigid need to control everything, they all tend to overextend themselves in meeting others' needs. Across all types, there is a lack of healthy boundaries, leading them to work and accommodate at the expense of their own well-being. This imbalance creates resentment, as they neglect their own needs in favor of the needs of others.

Parenting as an Extension of Serial Fixing

Parenthood naturally presents countless opportunities for those with serial fixer tendencies to structure and make decisions on behalf of their children. Infants, who rely entirely on their parents, provide fertile ground for the serial fixer's need to organize and control. These well-intentioned efforts often stem from a desire to ensure the well-being of the child, yet they can also be fueled by external perceptions and societal pressures about what it means to be a "good" parent. The need for validation, coupled with the overwhelming stream of choices that parenting presents, can exacerbate the serial fixer's drive to control and manage every aspect of their child's life.

As the parent-child relationship deepens, the challenges and decisions that arise contribute to the development of a unique family framework. Many parents are deeply motivated to be fully present and protect their children from hardships. This desire may stem from a need to break generational cycles of trauma or to provide a better life than the one they experienced. However, the line between healthy involvement and overcontrol is thin. Serial fixers, with their innate drive to caretake, may struggle to maintain this balance, often crossing into what can be perceived as controlling behavior—for instance, managing every aspect of their child's schedule or stepping in to resolve minor conflicts on their behalf.

As children grow and become more independent, the role of the parent inevitably shifts. For the serial fixer, this transition can be particularly challenging. The decreased need for their guidance, structure, or advice may feel like a threat to their sense of purpose, leading to feelings of displacement or obsolescence. While most parents aspire to raise strong, independent children, the reality of this independence can trigger an internal struggle for serial fixers, as they must adjust their expectations and sense of identity. As parents, we are in the business of raising adults, a task that requires us to embrace our evolving roles and let go of the need to fix every challenge they encounter.

Reframing their parental role and learning to **self-validate** the contributions they've made to their child's growth is crucial for serial fixers. However, if they fail to adapt to these evolving dynamics, they risk fostering **codependency** or resentment. The urgency to replicate past roles and maintain control over a child's life can lead to strained relationships and missed opportunities for both the parent and the child to grow and connect with their own individuality.

self-validate—Acknowledging and valuing one's efforts and process, whether internal or external. This practice involves actively supporting oneself, celebrating accomplishments, and reinforcing positive self-regard.

codependency—Relying on another person for emotional regulation, decision-making, or validation due to low self-trust or self-reliance. This dependence can create an imbalance in relationships, as it limits personal autonomy and self-assurance.

If you're reading this and thinking you missed the boat or are being incredibly self-critical, remember that that viewpoint might not be entirely fair—or true. This moment offers a chance to be compassionate with yourself. If you're going to critique your actions, also acknowledge what you did well as a parent and recognize any negative generational cycles you may have broken. Nearly every parent, at one time or another, feels like they've missed the mark, but there is always an opportunity to revisit those decisions or circumstances and consider what you would do differently now. It's not about self-blame or reassurance; rather, it's about recognizing that, at times, fear may have driven your actions, leading to control, mistrust, or choices you now regret. All is not lost; meaningful repair can happen when you validate these experiences, take ownership, and make efforts to reconnect. Apologize and share these realizations with your children to create a path forward.

Meet Tamara

Tamara hurried into my office, found a spot that suited her on the far end of the couch, and promptly handed me her intake paperwork. I asked her how she felt about being there, and without hesitation, she said she was fine and just wanted to talk about her middle child and how to help him. It was almost as if Tamara feared I would grade or evaluate her parenting abilities. She had three adult children and reassured me that she loved all of them and was proud of them. Her oldest was the high achiever, a rule follower, and had managed to make decisions that aligned with their family culture, expectations, and religious beliefs. The youngest was still trying to find her footing but was contagiously positive and had a charismatic personality. Tamara's sleepless nights and waves of intense guilt centered on her middle child. He was thirty, married, and currently unemployed.

Tamara went on to explain that drugs and alcohol had been an issue for her son since high school. He had always been moody and could switch on a dime, but he had a loving side that presented itself every so often. These interactions, however, were becoming fewer and farther between. His marriage was rocky, and violent altercations between him and his wife often ended with Tamara's involvement. He was struggling financially and claimed he needed more time to find a job he was passionate about. Tamara and her husband were in the middle of it all, desperately trying to feed him advice that would resonate with him and ignite some change. There was no doubt in my mind that her advice and ideas were sound but they were repeatedly ignored by her son or poorly executed. Tamara's frustration increased, and with it, so did her guilt.

I helped her identify the pattern I was seeing. She was frantically trying to solve the jigsaw puzzle and fill in the gaps, but she didn't have all the answers or information. When this occurs, the brain, especially one of a serial fixer, begins to urgently fill in the missing puzzle pieces by using the fixer's own memories, narratives, and viewpoints. This is the material that we have readily available, and we start to make others' problems about us—our failures, deficits, and poor decisions. The brain frantically tries to gain closure, and we are often left feeling anxious or uncomfortable when things are left in limbo or unresolved. Tamara's puzzle had gaps and needed to be complete, so she resorted to taking **false ownership** to achieve clarity.

false ownership—Assuming responsibility for other people's emotions or situations without clear evidence. This involves making assumptions instead of gathering factual information through open communication, which can lead to misunderstandings and unnecessary guilt.

I explained this to Tamara and shared that this cycle of puzzle solving doesn't lead to closure. Quite the opposite; this cycle fuels anxiety. The internal frenzy of filtering through memories, values, conversations, and decisions is a difficult train to stop. Tamara was losing sleep. Her ability to focus and complete tasks became overshadowed by both guilt and problem-solving for her son. *She* was carrying the emotional load. *She* was trying to navigate and steer but had little control over the decisions that were being made.

Her sense of failure as a parent consumed her: "When he gets better, I will get better." She was beginning to lose herself, and her self-care was steadily declining. She would receive reassurance from others who were close to the situation, but these temporary Band-Aids would peel quickly, and she would be back to problem-solving and punishing herself in a vicious cycle. I asked Tamara what would happen if she stopped giving her son advice. What if she refrained from problem-solving for him and tried to meet him where he currently was, even though it was painful? She was a bit defensive at first, fighting the notion back because she gave good advice and was approachable. I recognized her protective response, seeing that Tamara was putting a moat around her ability and identity as a parent. We talked about this, and I validated these fears. I saw her shoulders relax. I could see we were aligning and beginning to make progress.

We discussed the imbalance in her relationship with her son. We highlighted that she was carrying the emotional load and doing the work. He was able to retreat to her in times of high **stress** or chaos, and she was repeatedly picking up the pieces. As part of our plan moving forward, Tamara began to focus on two things. First, she would reframe herself as a supporter for her son rather than a solver of his problems. Second, she would lead with empathy and curiosity but provide the space necessary for her son to brainstorm and process his current predicaments as he was able. Rather than providing him with suggestions and telling him what to do, she would ask him what he planned to do or outline his next steps. This method would prevent her from internalizing and taking ownership for his problems while confidently letting him know she believed in him fully.

> **stress**—A natural response to external pressures or demands that feel overwhelming or threatening. Stress affects mood, health, self-care habits, and relationships, often resulting in physical and emotional strain.

Tamara took an active, supportive role in her son's hardships but did not attempt to absorb the responsibility and solely make it about her. As I continued to work with Tamara, I saw other aspects of her life gain more space. She shared more genuine happiness and had the energy to take care of herself and nurture other relationships in her life. The grief, sadness, and hardship of the situation remained, but the cycle of dependency was slowly losing its hold on her. Her son had taken a few meaningful steps forward, and Tamara was doing her best to nurture and support these decisions rather than judge them or control them.

Tamara's journey is a powerful example of how letting go of control and stepping back from the role of a fixer can lead to healthier relationships and personal well-being. By reframing herself as a supporter rather than a fixer, she was able to reclaim her own life and empower her son to take responsibility for his. This shift in perspective not only eased her anxiety but also created space for her son to grow and make sustainable decisions on his own.

Tamara's story serves as a reminder that the need to fix or control situations, especially those involving loved ones, often stems from our own anxieties and fears. However, fixing and controlling creates cycles of dependency and prevents the very growth and independence intended. By recognizing when to step back, set boundaries, and focus on supporting rather than controlling, we foster meaningful, authentic relationships and ensure we don't lose *ourselves* in the process.

How might you be assuming the role of a fixer in your own life? Are you carrying the emotional load for someone else? Are you trying to solve problems that aren't yours to solve? If so, don't fret, you're in the right place. You, along with many other serial fixers will learn how to shift your role from a solver to a supporter.

Repetitions

Throughout this book, I will refer to the term **reps** as a coping technique and essential practice. The phrase "get your reps in" became a guiding principle for me on the basketball court and soccer field during my youth, and it was further solidified during my time as a Division 1 athlete. My coaches used the phrase not only to motivate me and my teammates but also to challenge a rigid mindset that fixated on perfection or fueled

> **reps**—Short for "repetitions." Purposefully repeating a behavior or mindset to build confidence and self-trust, much like practicing a skill to gain mastery.

unrealistic expectations. Many of us were told growing up that practice makes perfect. "Get your reps in" is a similar saying but without the mention of perfection. Our bodies and minds must gain confidence and trust in our abilities to consistently deliver.

I learned early on that reps could also happen beyond the court. My dad encouraged me to tackle everyday challenges that felt uncomfortable but were invaluable in building my confidence. If there was a phone call to make—like arranging my own insurance as a new driver, scheduling appointments, or asking for help in a store when I was young—he'd push me to handle it myself, even when I felt nervous. When I struggled with performance anxiety in high school, he would listen for hours without stepping in to talk to my coach, as much as I may have wanted him to; instead, he encouraged me to have that conversation myself. These experiences taught me that these reps in everyday interactions are just as essential as physical practice.

Whether on the court, on the field, or in the game of life itself, getting your reps is an unfailing way to build confidence and mastery. In athletics, feats like running marathons require dedication, structure, and consistent practice. Most people aren't capable of running twenty-six miles without steadily growing toward the goal with practice. Now, if I were to tell someone that I hadn't worked out in any form for several months or even a year and then decided to run a marathon that coming weekend, it would be understandable if they had concerns about my ability to tackle that challenge. Not to say it couldn't be done, but if I shared that I had actually been training consistently, their confidence—and mine—in the situation would likely be much higher. When I've got my reps in, the chances of completing the challenge, enjoying it, and avoiding injury are far greater. The benefit of advanced training is that it provides your body and mind opportunities to work together, reset unnecessary doubts or fears, and build confidence and resilience. You prepare both your emotional mind and your body.

Reps play a similar role when it comes to our well-being and self-care. I have worked with many clients over the years with powerful roles in corporate life who subscribe to an urgent pace that involves multitasking, interruptions, and loose boundaries that prevent them from having adequate time for recovery and effective self-care. I hear a similar story they tell about vacation very often. When they finally have an upcoming trip or vacation, they can't wait to detach, replenish, and reconnect with others or a dormant part of themselves. The countdown has begun. The week leading up to the vacation is packed with extra to-dos and the delegation of added tasks to make time off truly count and break free. Stress is now higher, but it will all be worth it once vacation starts, right?

They arrive at their destination but experience an unexpected spike in anxiety, which they try to soothe at first by reassuring themselves that they are just transitioning and adjusting to a new place with a new pace. This works for the first day or two, but anxiety continues to occupy too much of their internal real estate. They find pockets of enjoyment and peace during their vacation but are also flooded with confusion and disappointment. They ask themselves, "Why am I so anxious? I'm in a beautiful location with nothing pressing to do!"

Afterward, I see them in my office feeling damaged, frustrated, and guilty for masking these uncomfortable feelings with alcohol or other unproductive coping mechanisms, which lead to even more exhaustion or detachment. There is nothing wrong with them. We both find that this connection makes logical sense when the scenario is broken down. When busy professionals only exercise and get reps for the high-stress, high-octane parts of their mind, those are the workouts the brain expects. When the workout suddenly changes polarity, their mind is woefully out of shape. They have no recent reps practicing peacefulness, presence, relaxation, and connection. Most clients were able to feel these things once before, but like muscles when not used for long periods, it will take consistent reps to improve their emotional shape. The good news is that the mind can build reps on both skills without needing to quit a job or take a long leave of absence. Athletes divide workouts by muscle group, giving each muscle group individual attention on a predictable cycle of work, rest, and then repeat. The mind is the same way, and later we will explore how you can mirror an athlete's formula for success with the body by learning how to access and rep your mind across more states and emotions.

"Get your reps in" is a way to motivate ourselves, but we must also accept that the first few reps will likely trigger uncomfortable feelings and thought patterns. This is normal and indicates that your amygdala, the part of your brain responsible for keeping you safe and alive, is working. At times, the amygdala is working way too hard, though, and it needs to be soothed and reassured. The more reps you get, the more you build confidence in your abilities. This is not unlike the days of soreness that follow working out a muscle for the first time after a long break. As you continue, what was once tangled in fear, doubt, or mistrust starts to shift, allowing you to embrace new practices or activities with greater ease and confidence.

Chapter 2

Emotional Hangovers

When you saw the word *hangover* in this chapter's title your mind might have instantly recalled a time when you overindulged, felt jet-lagged, or just woke up feeling like you were hit by a truck. For serial fixers, emotional hangovers are a common experience. Emotional hangovers are intense releases of feelings that occur after particularly stressful events or situations that require prolonged emotional energy or composure. You might wake up feeling drained and disoriented, even though the emotional effort has passed. The event or transition is over, but the accumulation of difficult emotions releases later. This phenomenon is perplexing because the wave of angst, anger, or exhaustion typically surfaces after the triggering event has ended or been resolved. Even when you've had time to prepare for an emotional challenge, the hangover can still occur. This is the body and mind's way of decluttering what you needed to suppress to endure a period of emotional challenge or hardship.

Emotional hangovers can feel like the crash that follows a caffeine overload. You might have felt energized and sharp at first, but as the buzz wears off, you're left feeling drained and jittery, maybe even a bit foggy. Similarly, when you've taken a risk or navigated a triggering event or conversation, the mind may need a respite period. You might feel more emotional or anxious. Reframing these hangover symptoms as your mind and body's attempt to clear the clutter and rebalance provides an opportunity to validate yourself and acknowledge the reps you've acquired.

During intense periods of emotional exertion—like an unexpected project at work or an unplanned visit from a high-maintenance family member—it's common to suppress certain emotions or parts of yourself to channel only what the situation needs. This helps you keep your mind focused as you navigate and endure the situation. While this tactic is effective, it burns emergency fuel that cannot last forever. Suppression takes work and involves pushing aside thoughts or emotions in order to give command only to the parts of yourself that will handle the challenge best. Whether you need to appear present, laid-back, strong, or engaging, these expressed qualities and behaviors mask underlying conflict, anxiety, or frustration—feelings that will eventually need release.

Once the event or interaction ends, you might experience a wave of exhaustion. This is the beginning of an emotional hangover. Processing and filtering even trivial social interactions becomes challenging. Sensitivity increases and feelings of vulnerability set in, often accompanied by impatience and becoming easily overwhelmed. This signals the aftermath of the internal fight where you struggled to silence your Inner-Critic (more on this struggle with the InnerCritic in chapter 3) and suppress hundreds of comments or statements.

Perhaps someone made an insensitive comment, or an intense conversation stirred up difficult emotions—the very ones you work hard to keep in check to maintain peace or stay in the good graces of others. These efforts can be exhausting but are part of the human experience. We are often called to adapt to situations even when they don't completely align with our views, moods, or objectives. This rapid mental filtering is necessary for daily engagement, comprehension, and collaboration, but it becomes detrimental when we are constantly reconfiguring and adapting to please others at the expense of our own well-being. This leaves us feeling depleted, with little to no space for our own needs. The disconnect grows and the negative effects are amplified as the internal clutter begins to interfere with our ability to rationalize and recharge. If this cycle becomes a normal pattern, we may turn to external quick fixes to soothe discomfort. Some of these methods are healthier than others, but all these external remedies miss addressing the real cause of pain. We might ignore signals of stress on body and mind as we focus on helping others, but we'll find that these emotional hangovers become a much more regular occurrence.

Imagine a day spent rushing from task to task—avoiding outbursts, meeting deadlines, and handling each adrenaline-fueled moment. Finally, you're in bed, and the day's demands are behind you. You'd think rest would come easily, right? But instead of acknowledging your efforts or planning time to process what just happened, you push down any lingering emotions and thoughts, convincing yourself it's simply not the right time to deal with them.

Yet in these moments of potential relaxation, those **suppressed** emotions resurface, seeking attention. Your body and mind view this as an opportunity to cleanse and declutter, disrupting your plan to escape and unwind.

> **suppression**—Temporarily setting aside thoughts or emotions to focus on the present moment. While suppression can be helpful in certain situations, relying on it too often without later processing can lead to emotional buildup.

As you lie down to sleep, hoping for a natural reset, you inevitably struggle. Thoughts about the day, last week, or perhaps overwhelming memories from middle school recycle themselves endlessly. The frustrating part is that your mind is nowhere near peak performance. The logical parts of your brain—the ones you rely on to set internal boundaries or suppress thoughts—are down for the count. You may have given in and had that glass of wine or two or used another substance as a "reward" or calming agent, hoping it would help you seamlessly transition into a calm state. This Band-Aid approach often replaces true reflection and internal decluttering, which are essential for encouraging a restful night's sleep.

Imagine a garden that is consistently tended and nurtured. It flourishes, creating a harmonious space for everything growing within it. But when abandoned and left to fend for itself, the garden can survive for a while, relying on external factors that, for a time, might even sustain it. Occasional rain or mild weather may disguise the lack of attention, making it hard to see the neglect. However, when conditions shift to something harsher, the plants and flowers begin to wilt, struggling to survive. Defenses weaken, and over time, without the needed care, the ecosystem is lost.

If garden images don't quite work for you, another helpful image related to this kind of emotional neglect is a concept I like to call a "suppression bubble." Suppression bubbles are emotions pocketed and stored in the body that must eventually be released. If they are not addressed intentionally—through therapy, self-care, or other supportive practices—the mind and body eventually take over, releasing the stored emotions in less structured ways to clear your internal clutter. This release can manifest in many forms, with common ones including exhaustion, intense irritability, anxiety, or a noticeable dip in mood.

Over the years, I've worked with many clients who were taught or learned on their own at a young age to suppress their feelings or rely on distractions instead of viewing their emotions as valuable data points to engage with. This approach can hinder their ability to build **self-trust** and avoid stagnation. The analogy of walking on

> **self-trust**—Confidence in one's own resilience and ability to recover. Self-trust involves understanding your motivations and making healthy decisions based on self-awareness.

eggshells comes to mind, describing what it's like to grow up in an environment where emotional turbulence is unpredictable and intense. In these situations, children quickly learn to suppress their needs, wants, and emotions, recognizing early on that there is no space for them.

For these individuals, emotional hangovers often manifest as anxiety when suppression continues over extended periods. Or a massive hangover will occur later, once the body and mind have reached their capacity. These are often personally or socially catastrophic and debilitating on many levels. Keeping with the image of a suppression bubble, imagine those bubbles settling into the cracks and crevices within us. When the number or size of suppression bubbles becomes too great, the body must intervene and find a time to release and rid itself of the accumulated burden and clutter.

Meet Carlos

Carlos was in his late sixties when we met and began working together. He celebrated a decade of sobriety after recently navigating a divorce and a few years of retirement. His days were now comparatively peaceful, free from competing in the rat race and the demands of a partnership. In our sessions, he expressed a desire to explore the parts of himself that had been "dormant" for decades and to check off items on his bucket list. However, as his pace slowed down and deadlines and accountability faded, he was overrun with anxiety, anger, sadness, and guilt. For decades, he had used alcohol as an escape, operating with a sense of urgency to distract himself from the abuse and neglect he endured as a child. His teenage years were traumatic and full of loss, but he was left to his own devices to cope and just move on. This is where distraction and disconnect entered the picture. He stumbled numbly through life, numb to the pain, hoping to find peace and presence in retirement.

Unfortunately, his mind was out of shape, lacking the self-trust necessary for accessing this level of peacefulness and presence. Carlos was flooded with the repetitive release of his suppression bubbles, many of which had been created in his youth and claimed real estate for decades. As life's demands lessened and his body and mind recognized the shift, they seized the opportunity to release and declutter. This emotional cleanse manifested in the form of anxiety, shame, anger, and depressive symptoms that had been accumulating for years.

Carlos's story illustrates a powerful truth: When we suppress emotions and rely on distractions to navigate through life, those emotions don't just disappear—they accumulate, waiting for a moment when we finally slow down. For Carlos, as with many others who will experience the same, retirement brought a flood of unresolved emotions.

Today's urgency culture leaves little room for processing and the digestion of information, thought, and emotion. Once you have capitulated to the pressures to "be on" and "produce, produce, produce," it becomes incredibly challenging to integrate pauses and adequate times for rejuvenation. Amid overstimulation and distractions, somewhere time must be set aside to address intense reactions and uncomfortable emotions. Some bubbles are bigger than others. Some sit deeper within us. No matter their composition, these bubbles have information we need to process. If we don't set aside a time, a place, and a method to do this, they'll bombard us later, with the added penalty of not understanding why we feel run-down, sad, or anxious.

This pattern isn't unique to Carlos. Many of us, like Carlos, may find ourselves out of practice when it comes to being present and dealing with our emotions head-on. As we go through life's demands, we often push them aside, hoping they'll resolve themselves later. But when life quiets down or changes, those suppressed emotions surface, sometimes overwhelming us and leaving us with emotional hangovers.

Emotional hangovers can manifest as meltdowns, an overwhelming need for solitude, or sheer exhaustion. During periods of repetitive high stress, the onset of illness or physical injury might be your body's way of signaling a hangover. Growing up, I didn't get sick more often than the average child, but I remember calling my mother from college one day, feeling crummy and seeking sympathy. She offered a few quick, motherly nursing tips to ease my cold symptoms. She also pointed out a pattern she had noticed. Whenever basketball season ended and I finally had some downtime, I would get sick. As I listened to her elaborate, I realized she was right. It was as if my body and mind recognized the intense pace I had maintained, and getting sick became a way of forcing me to pause. My body couldn't sustain the perpetual cycle, and by March, I was running on fumes, neglecting time for recovery and rejuvenation. This experience extends beyond the physical; if we fail to prioritize self-care and maintain a connection to ourselves, we risk emotional burnout, emotional hangovers, or turning to unhealthy methods of self-soothing.

The pressure to consistently set aside your needs and boundaries for the sake of accommodating others or a situation primes you for burnout and emotional hangovers. This setup hinders your ability to be present and authentically connect not only with yourself but also with others. New parents quickly discover the transformative benefits of a bedtime routine. It provides a moment to debrief, unwind, complete tasks validating the day, and mindfully prepare for a reset. When executed successfully, it becomes a source of accomplishment for the caregiver and an opportunity for self-care. However, it's often crowded with multitasking, consumption, or distractions that interfere with the necessary window to process, reflect, and unplug.

Serial fixers given a task or challenge typically rise up to complete it. They resort to quick fixes which they can recognize easily, and they navigate their lives borrowing others' expectations as their main source of structure. This leads to an internal disconnect. Progressing through hardship without authentic check-ins to reflect on progress results in a lack of accomplishment and peace, despite the fixers' expectation that they're getting the fulfillment they desire.

The pleaser within us wants to be seen as successful in the eyes of others, striving for validation, a sense of belonging, and fulfillment. The desire to prove our worthiness, be aware of others' needs, and shield them from discomfort is admirable, but not in an endless pursuit. When taken too far, it backfires, becoming a major cause of burnout and confusion. The serial fixer often asks themselves, "I am trying so hard. Why is this not working? Why am I not getting back all that I put in?"

If our relationships aren't balanced, and if our efforts to serve others don't lead to true connection, we can find ourselves exhausted and disconnected. We try so hard to please others and give constantly, with a prevailing hope that fulfillment is imminent. Without boundaries and space for self-reflection and validation, this recipe is incomplete. The body and mind become depleted and can no longer accommodate suppression bubbles. Furthermore, we miss opportunities to "be real" with ourselves in the moment.

Are you honoring your values and making space for yourself while fulfilling others' needs and checking off boxes?

While we all have to push through and conform to expected behaviors in certain situations—such as a family event that requires charm, eye contact, and combatting anxiety—pausing to check in with ourselves prevents discomfort or painful drama later.

Validating this effort and acknowledging the recovery that may be required, along with creating downtime or a debriefing session following the event, is a form of self-care. Clients nearly always report an unexpected rush of emotions afterward. This is normal if you make a prolonged effort to overcome discomfort and hesitation.

In the chapters that follow, we'll explore a powerful tool for self-discovery and maintenance—**self-check-ins**. These are moments of intentional reflection where you pause to assess your emotional well-being, identify patterns, and make adjustments. For example, imagine you notice a consistent dip in your mood on certain days. During a self-check-in, you explore the circumstances surrounding these dips. Perhaps they are related to specific activities, people, interactions, or even environmental factors. Armed with this awareness, you can proactively implement coping strategies, whether it's scheduling moments of self-care, seeking support, or adjusting your routine to address some of your suppression bubbles. Silencing or judging your dips in mood or energy fuels negative self-talk and perpetuates an all-or-nothing mentality. You'll learn to incorporate self-check-ins into your routine, providing opportunities for validation, data collection, and shifts to insert coping skills or reframe. The goal is not to check off boxes but to be genuine with the efforts and motivations driving these desires.

> **self-check-in**—A mindful pause in a person's day to evaluate their current thoughts, emotions, and physical sensations. This process helps increase self-awareness without judgment or a need to fix anything immediately.

These moments of deliberate reflection act as a compass and mark critical waypoints in our journey, guiding us through our emotions and thought patterns. As the famous saying goes, "know thyself"—a timeless reminder that self-awareness is the foundation for growth and understanding. Imagine having the ability to anticipate and address emotional dips before they become patterns, much like an experienced navigator adjusting course to cut through the waves with wind at their back.

Self-check-ins are not just about identifying the nuances of our emotional landscape but also about crafting practical strategies and structure. Picture our journey as a road map to self-awareness, providing the insights needed to proactively steer through the complexities of daily life. The goal is to authentically engage with our efforts and motivations propelling us forward.

Serial fixers can experience emotional hangovers often. The lingering feelings of fatigue, overload, and disconnect arise when we prioritize others' needs over our own. It's essential to recognize that constantly striving for external validation and attempting to meet every expectation leaves us feeling empty and exhausted. By establishing boundaries and embracing our own needs, we can reclaim our well-being and foster authentic connections without sacrificing ourselves in the process. You'll learn to do that here. Remember, taking the time to process and reflect isn't a sign of weakness but a vital step toward nurturing our mental health and ensuring that we can genuinely support others without depleting ourselves.

Chapter 3

Aligning with Your InnerPleaser, InnerRescuer, and InnerCritic

In this chapter, we will explore the underlying reasons behind the recurring patterns and tendencies of a serial fixer. You have likely already recognized your serial fixer patterns—that's why you picked up this book! Now let's delve into why you keep repeating them. I will introduce three aspects of our inner selves: the InnerPleaser, the InnerRescuer, and the InnerCritic. These aspects exist in nearly all of us but in varying degrees. For some of us, one of our inner parts will overperform and mask the other two. Honoring, understanding, and creating space for each part helps us gain a deeper self-connection and fosters a more balanced inner dialogue.

I had a client years ago who compared her inner chaos to an orchestra. She described it as if each section of the orchestra had its own agenda: The strings yearned for delicate, emotional melodies; the brass was eager to play bold, heroic tunes; and the percussion wanted to keep things lively with a thunderous beat. She felt like the stressed-out conductor, frantically trying to harmonize these diverse impulses. The chaos was overwhelming and at times made her question her sanity. If this resonates with you, know that you're not alone.

To make this analogy clearer, imagine that the strings represent your InnerPleaser—always striving to keep others happy and avoid conflict. The brass symbolizes your rescuer—deeply attuned to others' emotions and eager to support them. The percussion embodies your InnerCritic—constantly evaluating and pushing you to improve. Understanding how these parts interact can help you manage internal conflicts more effectively.

As you continue reading, I encourage you to keep an open mind and take notes. Your goal is to become more aware of, and "intimate" with, these key parts of your inner self. The InnerPleaser, InnerRescuer, and InnerCritic are not distinct personality types but rather aspects of your experience. For example, your InnerPleaser might drive you to say yes when you'd prefer to decline, while your InnerRescuer might make you feel overwhelmed by others' emotions, and your InnerCritic might fuel self-doubt. Some of you may find it easy to relate to these parts because you interact with or attempt to suppress them frequently. Others might connect with only one or two, feeling the others are dormant or even nonexistent.

Recognizing the motivations and protective strategies of these inner aspects can provide valuable insights into your behavior. By increasing your self-awareness, you can start to appreciate the roles they have played in your life and learn to manage them in a way that supports your well-being. For instance, acknowledging your InnerCritic's intention to push you toward growth can help you use it constructively rather than letting it undermine your confidence.

Gaining insight into the motives and tendencies of these inner parts helps you understand what they represent and advocate for, as well as how they have influenced your actions over the years. Our goal is not to dismiss them but rather to learn how to work with them. This is a key component of the Internal Family Systems (IFS) model, which is a therapeutic modality utilized by thousands of clinicians around the world. Building from IFS, we will explore how certain parts of you interact and influence your behavior. The focus will be on recognizing and aligning with the three specific aspects—the InnerPleaser, InnerRescuer, and InnerCritic—in a way that feels practical and accessible. As you read on, you'll learn some practical ways to help these components of you coexist peacefully and amplify one another. The more you understand and appreciate their roles, the easier it will be to create a more balanced and intentional way of living.

The InnerPleaser

Saying no to other people is not a comfortable practice for most of us. Our InnerPleaser is driven by a strong motivation to help and accommodate others, even if it means neglecting our own needs. This pleasing aspect of us seeks to keep the peace and protect others from discomfort, avoiding situations where we might be perceived as selfish or uncaring. This part would prefer us to take on the burden or continue accommodating rather than face conflict or interfere with someone's opinion of us.

Those with strong InnerPleasers anticipate, serve, and accommodate others, allowing external needs to dictate their decision-making and sense of connection. Empathy kicks in strongly and prematurely, leading them to shower others in accommodation even before a request is made. These individuals are empaths in overdrive. Their unchecked emotional expenditure leads to exhaustion, being taken advantage of, or developing a dependency on others' approval.

This pattern of behavior can permeate all types of relationships. People with strong InnerPleasers prioritize the needs of others so much that their primary framework for how they structure their lives is based upon their ability to serve others. They derive their sense of worthiness from meeting these needs. As a result, their own self-care and self-reflection are pushed well beneath what they give to others.

Our InnerPleaser neglects internal connection and validation, sacrificing reps in exchange for spending energy on others around us. Regular self-check-ins are either forgotten or never implemented. This lack of self-connection has a *poison in the well* effect as space that would normally be used for internal reflection is instead filled up with symptoms of anxiety. Over time, resentment builds, as it is challenging to survive in a world where our identity and value are solely defined by others' needs and affirmations.

Individuals with dominant InnerPleasers also struggle with voicing their opinions, setting boundaries, or expressing genuine feelings. When they finally verbalize their needs, these expressions can be misconstrued as combative, ungrateful, or selfish—largely because assertiveness is rare in their behavior and its sudden onset is disorienting. Fear of conflict, combined with the infrequency of asserting themselves, leads to InnerPleasers avoiding openly communicating their needs or discontent.

In many cultures, harmony is valued over individual assertion, making it even more challenging for our InnerPleaser to navigate conversations involving conflict or personal boundaries. The unspoken expectation to avoid discomfort inadvertently places a premium on maintaining the status quo, even if it means suppressing one's authentic voice. Consequently, verbalizing anger or disapproval becomes an unconventional response, met with raised eyebrows or perplexed glances.

Those with dominant InnerPleasers engage in an intricate dance of restraint, aiming to achieve connection or unity but unintentionally stifling the richness of diverse perspectives. The challenge lies not only in expressing themselves but in pushing back against the expectation that asserting their needs will be seen by others as an affront. Cultural and gender factors may contribute to people-pleasing tendencies, as societal expectations and norms shape these behaviors differently across individuals.

When conflicting sentiments go unaddressed, a cycle of misunderstandings thrives, and the genuine intent behind assertive expressions often gets lost in the fear of deviating from the norm. A cultural reset is needed—one that values candid conversations, where differing opinions are seen not as threats but as catalysts for growth and understanding. Until then, breaking free from the shackles of conformity may be difficult, leaving many hesitant to explore their inner truths and truly connect with themselves.

Navigating the delicate balance between honoring your InnerPleaser and InnerRescuer, while also prioritizing your needs and carving out space for rejuvenation, can be a nuanced challenge. However, it is essential for those committed to well-being and showing up authentically in life. Learning to embrace external validation while understanding it doesn't solely define self-worth connection is crucial. Shifting energy inward and focusing on internal validation enhances self-connection and brings greater peace, presence, and balanced, healthy interactions.

Meet Neve

Neve had been an educator for over a decade and was recently moved into the role of head teacher for her department. She led by example and was now someone that new and experienced teachers alike could go to for support and guidance. Neve reached out to me when her anxiety became constant in her day. She was juggling her role as an educator amid the COVID-19 pandemic and desperately wanted to become pregnant and start her family. She and her spouse had been trying to conceive for two years, and this weighed heavily on her heart. The pressure she put on herself was intense. Logically, she grasped that much of this process was out of her control. Emotionally, though, she blamed herself. She was angry with her body, and questions of whether she was worthy of becoming a mother kept her up at night. She was incredibly organized and thorough, and she researched excessively about ways to improve her chances of conception. She was bombarded by these thought patterns and the emotions they triggered. Her anxious thoughts gained power and took up the spaces once occupied by her ability to be present and feel fulfilled by her various roles.

It was evident early on that Neve had a high level of self-awareness and empathy. Her new leadership role was a source of pride, but she wasn't able to create and hold the necessary boundaries it required. Neve, like many educators I had worked with, was motivated by an innate drive to serve and help. She was available to her colleagues and the parents of her students twenty-four seven. Other teachers would filter through her classroom with questions or seeking reassurance or structure. Neve prided herself on giving sound advice, completing tasks for others, or ironing out minor conflicts brought by her team. She was a doer, a solver, and a fixer. Unfortunately, her routine did not include time for rejuvenation, reflection, or recovery. There was no end in sight and the emotional conversations that once only monopolized her work hours were now creeping into her downtime.

Her InnerPleaser was fierce and kept her on a path to avoid disappointing others or triggering guilt. She was an educator and a lead teacher. She told herself it was her duty to help and be available. Neve knew the words *boundary* and *presence* and spoke to her students about them. Despite feeling resentment for the distractions created by the needs and asks of others, she welcomed them. They provided a needed escape from her negative self-talk, the voices that sabotaged her ability to be present and prevented her from any form of self-validation (more on this later in this chapter). Focusing on other people's issues was exhausting for her but served as a mental detour, providing her with distractions from her own anxiety.

Neve could no longer access the positive energy and attentiveness that her students had grown to expect each day. She explained that she felt a growing level of resentment and an almost crippling envy of other women who were able to be mothers. It was also becoming evident that the new teachers who initially asked for only morsels of guidance had now grown dependent on her. They chose not to problem solve for themselves and instead came to Neve to structure, encourage, or fix. She began questioning if her generosity was being taken advantage of and if others viewed her not as a resource but as a crutch, or perhaps the someone who could take things off their plates entirely. She needed a boundary reset, but this would require space, consistency, and a higher level of self-awareness. Neve would have to reevaluate her frameworks and face her anxieties directly.

I challenged Neve to explore beneath the stressors and distractions that were monopolizing her energy levels and leaving her feeling like she was on a hamster wheel day after day. It was almost as if she was anticipating change but forgetting that she needed to be deliberate about her actions and boundaries if she really wanted shifts to occur. Growing up, even from a young age, she was the peacekeeper. Evenings in her childhood household featured frequent and intense arguments between her parents, fueled by her father's alcohol use disorder. Her siblings looked to her for guidance and comfort. She learned early in life that there was very little room for error or difficult feelings. Her mother seemed to always be at capacity, and her father repeatedly demonstrated that he was not emotionally available and only connected with his children if there was a success to celebrate. His standards were high, mirroring the setup he experienced as a child: "Keep your head up and shove the ugly down."

Neve's high level of emotional intelligence served her well through this period. She could anticipate the moods of her family members and make adjustments in advance to avoid conflict or to ensure she didn't miss an opportunity to engage positively with her mother or father. Seeing how this strategy mitigated problems at home, she replicated these patterns with her friends and teachers. The occasional praise from other adults was like candy to Neve. She craved it, needed it, and extended herself to receive affirmation from others, usually leaving her feeling isolated or exhausted.

Neve found herself in several relationships that left her feeling confused, used, and hopeless. Her energy wasn't being returned or replicated. In sessions, we began to uncover the true motivators and fears that drove her InnerPleaser to overperform and dictate her decisions. This part of her held too much space, too much power, and it was evident that she didn't trust that anyone other than her InnerPleaser could navigate life and everything that crossed her path. Thanks to Neve and our therapeutic work, a phrase was born: "Be a supporter, not a solver." This one phrase was the foundation for the work that Neve needed to adopt a new mindset and structure for her relationships with others and herself.

I acknowledged with Neve that introducing new boundaries, especially with her colleagues, would be an uncomfortable task at first. She should anticipate confusion and questions that will trigger her sense of guilt and challenge her sense of worth.

What if people think I'm being mean or difficult?
What if people become upset and blame me for not helping?
What if people stop coming to me for help altogether?
What if people see me as lazy?

These questions fueled her anxieties and deepened her fears about her struggle to conceive. She often wondered if she had waited too long to try or if her dedication to work was to blame. Neve was scared. She knew what needed to change, but the habits ingrained from an early age and her fear of rejection fixed her into a state of mental paralysis, unable to make the necessary shifts.

I challenged Neve to carve out a small but consistent amount of time each day for herself. This would be a time to check in and to examine the roles and relationships in her life that left her feeling overwhelmed. She needed to identify and get to know what parts of her were leading when they shouldn't and prioritize where shifts could be made. We created frameworks and templates to assist her in processing these daily check-ins, starting with the core areas she identified as the most difficult to navigate:

Who or what is causing me to feel overwhelmed today?
Is my energy depleted or scattered?
What feelings are triggered by this person or experience?
What needs to be true for me to feel supported today?
What expectations need to shift for me to feel supported?
What boundaries need to be introduced or reimplemented for me to feel balanced and fulfilled?
What steps do I need to take today to regain control of my energy and my time?
What is one thing I can do today that nurtures my well-being?

With these guiding questions, Neve could start each day from a place of self-awareness and intention. She learned to recognize when her InnerPleaser was taking over and to step back, refocus, and realign with her needs. This practice helped her to regain a sense of control and to balance her dedication to others with a commitment to herself. By taking small, deliberate steps, she began to rebuild her the connection with herself, creating a stronger foundation for navigating the complexities of her life with greater ease and confidence.

Ultimately, our InnerPleaser often struggles to say no, preferring to take on burdens or accommodate others rather than risk conflict or damaging our image. This drive to maintain peace and protect others from discomfort, even at our own expense, can lead to a pattern of anticipating and serving others' needs, allowing these needs to dictate our decisions and sense of connection. While empathy and care are admirable, they can result in exhaustion, being taken advantage of, or a dependency on others' approval.

This mindset can pervade all relationships, with our InnerPleaser often deriving self-worth from solely meeting others' needs. Consequently, self-care and reflection are neglected, amplifying anxiety as internal validation fades away. Our inability to voice opinions or set boundaries compounds the issue, as our InnerPleasers fear that asserting ourselves will be seen as selfish or combative. Societal norms that prioritize harmony over individual assertion further reinforce this hesitancy, leading to a cycle where genuine self-expression is stifled, and misunderstandings thrive.

Navigating the delicate balance between honoring our InnerPleaser while prioritizing self-care is challenging but essential. We must learn to understand that external validation does not solely define our self-worth. By shifting focus inward and cultivating internal validation, we can improve our relationship with ourselves and foster healthier, more balanced interactions.

The InnerRescuer

The InnerRescuer is motivated by empathy, transforming sensitivity into a powerful tool for understanding and connecting with those around us. Empathy, rooted in active listening and presence, allows the InnerRescuer to quickly gauge others' feelings. With heightened perceptiveness, the InnerRescuer connects deeply on an emotional level, often experiencing others' emotions as if they were their own. While empathy is a complex trait that varies in intensity, it shapes how we sense and decode the emotions around us. We may focus more on people's emotional states than on the details of our environment, using our ability to interpret facial expressions to assess mood and intentions. This skill can help us avoid conflicts and connect with others in ways that ease social anxiety.

For instance, at a social event our InnerRescuer might naturally gravitate toward someone who appears lonely or anxious, offering comfort and support. Although this fosters deep connections, it also means we are continuously absorbing and processing the emotional states of others, which can be overwhelming.

Our InnerRescuer processes facial expressions and words and relates them to our own experiences, allowing us to understand others on a deep emotional level. When the InnerRescuer is overperforming, it's heightened empathy can lead to taking false ownership of others' experiences and hardships. While empathy enables us to validate others' feelings effectively, excess empathy can lead to distress if we **internalize** these emotions and let them influence our own state of being.

> **internalize**—The process of taking in beliefs, values, or feelings from others and making them part of how a person thinks and feels. This can happen when someone absorbs what people around them say or believe, which sometimes leads to blaming themselves for things that aren't their fault. It often occurs when you make assumptions or don't have all the important information, resulting in unhealthy self-blame or attempts to make sense of situations based on your ego.

This tendency to internalize others' emotions is linked to specific neurological processes. For example, research by

Matthew D. Lieberman in his book *Social: Why Our Brains Are Wired to Connect* (2013) supports the argument that the InnerRescuer is associated with heightened activity in brain regions related to social cognition and emotional regulation, such as the anterior insula and the mirror neuron system. Additionally, research by Tania Singer, a leader in social neuroscience, demonstrates that these same regions are active when we empathize with others' emotions, highlighting the challenge of maintaining emotional boundaries. These brain regions help us vividly simulate and understand the emotional experiences of others but also challenge the maintenance of our emotional boundaries.

This dynamic is called the "ego filter," which does not mean egocentrism but rather highlights how we internalize and compare experiences to assess our own worth. This filter can induce fear and anxious thoughts, stemming from the uncertainty of how others perceive us. Even when a topic has no direct connection, our InnerRescuer may wonder if it reflects on us in some way.

The InnerRescuer can create intense pressure to soothe or fix others' problems, leading to self-sabotage and burnout. It's crucial for us to develop strategies to manage our sensitivity and set healthy boundaries. Practices such as mindfulness, self-reflection, and seeking support from trusted individuals can be invaluable.

The persistent "need" to fix and solve others' problems is what leads us to be serial fixers, compelled to resolve issues for those around us while neglecting our own needs. Regularly checking in with yourself, assessing your emotional state, and setting intentions can help maintain balance. Techniques like deep breathing, grounding exercises, and breaks from emotionally charged environments are also beneficial for recharging and preserving well-being.

Understanding and managing our rescuer tendencies is fundamental for our well-being and for fostering meaningful, balanced relationships. By recognizing our strengths and challenges, we can navigate our emotional world with greater ease and resilience, leading to more fulfilling and sustainable connections with others. Shifting from a mindset of fixing to one of supporting allows us to maintain empathy without sacrificing our own health, embodying the principle of "Support, Don't Solve" to create healthier and more authentic interactions.

Meet Daniel

Daniel was one of my first clients. I was twenty-four, fresh out of graduate school, and had landed my first job as a therapist with the Travis County Juvenile Probation Department in Austin, Texas. My caseload consisted of adolescents on probation. Some were detained in correctional facilities and participated in correctional programs while others lived at home, attended school, and met the requirements of their probation while participating in individual and family therapy with me.

Daniel was thirteen years old. He lived with his older brother and had a younger sister who was still a toddler. His mother struggled to keep a job, and most of our conversations eventually led to discussing her past trauma and latest breakup. Daniel didn't know his father. When he talked about his mother's ex-boyfriends, he would grit his teeth and shut down. As a young clinician, I recognized the intensity and complexity of the case but didn't quite know where to start. I had been taught to establish rapport, which I believe had happened. It was a challenge, but he began to open up and share more of his story and what was happening in his life.

I explored the grief associated with his absent father and the anger he felt toward his mother. On one occasion, he was telling me about a missing assignment at school and how his teacher responded to his lack of organization. He continued, expressing his frustration with his mom for never being home and making him watch his sister and then began to share his "one little mistake" that led to probation. His tears welled up. Anger fueled his tone. I was encouraged with the breakthrough but terrified about how to respond. I was being pulled by empathy and guilt. I couldn't directly relate to Daniel's situation, but I could empathize and understand how and why he felt the way he did. I knew that anger was the easiest emotion for him to express and that it had been the one most commonly modeled for him.

The guilt I felt was exacerbated by the contrast between my childhood and Daniel's. Growing up in a stable suburban household with supportive parents, my experiences were unlike his. As I navigated my empathy and guilt, I found myself stuck on how to "fix" his situation. I encouraged him and highlighted his strengths while scrambling to find the right options and coping techniques to share. Despite my best intentions, this approach only led to Daniel feeling overwhelmed and eventually shutting down completely. The safe space I created vanished and was replaced with my own discomfort and a misguided need to solve the problem.

This experience with Daniel illuminates a vital lesson about serial fixer tendencies. My interest in solving his problems stemmed from a place of empathy but ultimately proved counterproductive. The pressure to fix other people's problems can originate in personal guilt or cultural expectations, rather than a genuine effort to see someone conquer their struggles. The cultural component, where fixing is often seen as the ultimate goal, influenced my approach and intensified my internal struggle.

I continued to work with Daniel, eventually repairing our relationship. Through supervision and self-reflection, I learned the importance of creating a safe and consistent space for clients rather than imposing solutions. This shift from "fixing" to "supporting" allowed me to engage with clients more authentically, aligning my empathy to curiosity rather than to pressure. It became evident that my role was to empower clients to process and explore their feelings rather than to solve their problems.

Once I embraced this approach, it not only transformed my practice with clients but also enriched my personal relationships. By focusing on creating space and fostering authentic connections, I moved away from the serial fixer mindset and found a more sustainable and impactful way to support those around me. This shift underscored the need to address both personal and cultural influences to effectively navigate the challenges of empathy and boundary setting in professional and personal contexts.

The InnerCritic

I have yet to meet someone who doesn't feel insecure from time to time. Whether it's friends, clients of all ages, or high-powered CEOs, we are all working to navigate self-doubts and find a way to quiet the inner voices that question our worth. Our inner aspect whose main objective is to shield us from failure, discomfort, and isolation is our InnerCritic. The InnerCritic's role is to keep us safe, aiming to avoid negative judgment and the risk of falling behind. It craves external validation. When this part of us begins to overperform, anxiety tends to spike, perfectionistic tendencies express more strongly, and we find it increasingly difficult to give ourselves grace.

We should express gratitude for this aspect of ourselves for its intense role in keeping us from stagnating and missing out, as well as helping us live our lives to the fullest. However, the InnerCritic often takes on the voice of a demanding, critical, even shaming parent, coach, or teacher. This voice sometimes wants more than you can give and pushes you in a way that turns negative. These inner, critical voices are trying to protect us from falling behind or failing. Yet they often echo voices of authority figures who were one-sided and driven by self-interest, focused on preserving their image and conquering at all costs.

Our InnerCritic is accountable for ensuring that we progress and compete. It perpetuates a survival of the fittest mentality and strives to help us fit in just enough while standing out through our strengths. Many of my clients feel the presence of their InnerCritic when they make a mistake, lose control, or overindulge. When our InnerCritic is overpowered, our inner dialogue thickens with shame, clouding our gentler and forgiving psychology. The InnerCritic is also responsible for burnout and the inability to transition and recover effectively.

When I began speaking to larger audiences, I could feel an internal war brewing between my InnerRescuer and InnerCritic. I've always been a risk-taker, but as my professional work pivoted from counseling teens to speaking to groups of leaders and executives at multibillion-dollar companies, my InnerCritic came alive. Early in my speaking career, as I scrolled through the website of a company that had hired me, I started to feel intimidated. This company was staffed with experienced and professional mentors—most of whom were at least twenty-five years older than me and predominantly white men who had run successful businesses for decades. I questioned what they could possibly learn from me and whether they'd even listen.

Thankfully, my InnerRescuer quickly perked up, as it tends to do when self-defeating thoughts arise, offering me a much-needed pep talk. It reminded me that I'd overcome huge challenges before, whispering confidence and conjuring memories of times when I'd felt strong and capable. It called on my resilience, built over years, and reminded me of the reps I'd earned in other areas of life. With its presence, I felt a shift: I was reminded of what it was like to stand tall and believe in myself. My InnerRescuer nudged me toward a mindset of "fake it till you make it," but with a steady determination to see it through until I achieved my goal.

As I regained my balance, I stopped the endless scrolling and refocused on what I knew and what I wanted to share with the group. However, despite this internal pep talk, my InnerCritic wasn't ready to sit down quietly. A few weeks later, I was scheduled to facilitate a workshop on burnout for a financial services group. I could feel my heart rate accelerate and beads of sweat form as the session began. The percussion in my orchestra changed its beat and self-doubt began to creep in again.

What if I'm not ready for this?
What if my material isn't good enough?
What if they ask me a question I can't answer?
What if I look or sound like an idiot?
Did I wear the right outfit?

These questions and fears were not new to me. I had felt similar sensations, but this InnerCritic was fiercely strong and attacked my discomfort. It was promoting perceived consequences of failure and serving up persistent reminders that I was being challenged in an unfamiliar situation. To my InnerCritic, this was serious. I've learned to borrow and build on tenets of the IFS model in situations like these. The method encourages making an effort to understand this critical and doubtful voice rather than silence or avoid it, which seemed to only fuel its cyclical nature and amplify its power. My InnerCritic was determined to protect me at the expense of trusting my efforts to deliver, unscathed, unharmed, and emotionally intact. I began to pay more attention and learned my InnerCritic wanted me to succeed but wasn't convinced I could handle rejection or setbacks. It was up to me to convince my InnerCritic otherwise.

My speaking ritual before events began to look a bit different. I almost expected and welcomed my InnerCritic to show up. Sometimes it would greet me days before my speech, criticizing the fact that I hadn't gotten enough sleep and feeding me scenarios where I'd be exhausted and low on energy. Most of the time, though, it would show up about thirty minutes before I went on stage. My inner dialogue with my InnerCritic now goes something like this: "I thought you might show up. Thanks for being here and for all your efforts over the years to protect me. I want to remind you that we are not in danger, and we have had several reps at this point speaking to groups. We accepted this opportunity and really enjoy educating, supporting, and challenging our audiences. It also helps me grow. I want you to stick around, of course, but you're working too hard. Can you please take a break so that some of the other parts responsible for my confidence, recall, humor, and energy can have some space?"

This conversation took practice, and yes, it felt awkward at first! However, over time my InnerCritic began responding differently, and its level of trust in me has significantly grown. Of course, there are times when it still comes on like an avalanche, especially when I have an elevated level of stress and am not taking care of the basics as well as I should. My InnerCritic knows what it takes to sustain all my interests and commitments and has been with me since elementary school when I signed up for every club and tried to do it all. It knows me well and aims to protect my balance. I am a recovering perfectionist and learn by doing. My InnerCritic is constantly there to remind me of the importance of recovery and to access my resilience and grit to keep those feelings familiar, even if they come in different forms depending on the stage or chapter of life I am in.

I combined these cognitive techniques with physical actions I had learned as a Division 1 athlete, creating a powerful synergy that helped me counterbalance the mental chatter. I focused on making myself as big as possible, intentionally taking up space to ground myself. This involved flexing my muscles, doing a few push-ups, and listening to music that brought back memories of stepping onto the court before a big game with my teammates, all driven by an unrelenting desire to win. Internally, we were probably a bit unsure, nervous, or intimidated, but we knew that those thoughts and that energy were neither helpful nor needed. If we couldn't fully overpower it emotionally, we'd let our bodies convince our minds. The emotions we were feeling were protective, but the trust we had in each other, ourselves, and the countless hours of practice deserved more space.

I've continued to use this mindset throughout my life. Not every situation is conducive to push-ups or flexing my muscles, but I can walk tall, hold my head high, and enter a room with the attitude that I can handle whatever comes my way. My mind follows suit, drawing from my **resilience bank**. I remind myself that I've felt discomfort like this before. It might not be comfortable, but I survived it then—and I will now too. But no matter how much I work to center

> **resilience bank**—A personal reserve of experiences and "reps" a person has built over time, providing a source of motivation, clarity, grit, and resilience. It's the mental and emotional strength they can draw upon during challenging moments to persevere and thrive.

myself, the doubt and fear always seem to pop up right before a big moment.

Transitioning from understanding our inner parts and how they influence our interactions, we can see how these dynamics play out in real-world scenarios. One of the most significant challenges comes when we are faced with situations that test our confidence and self-belief. Just as we need to manage our InnerRescuer tendencies, we must also learn to navigate the internal dialogues that arise when we step into new or intimidating environments.

Imposter Syndrome and Our InnerCritic

Imposter syndrome is the antagonizing thought or fear that you are not capable, worthy, or good enough to fulfill a certain role or be included in a group. It is not classified as a psychological disorder but rather a mindset that develops from our insecurities, often fueled by a relentless InnerCritic. This InnerCritic perpetuates doubt, leading to self-sabotage and heightened anxiety, driven by a strong need for others to validate you and your status or abilities. Once thought to predominantly affect women, imposter syndrome can affect anyone, particularly during major life transitions when unpredictability is high.

> **imposter syndrome**—A recurring feeling of inadequacy and self-doubt often marked by fears of being "discovered" as incompetent. These thoughts can lead to insecurity, anxiety, and negatively impacted confidence and self-assurance.

The InnerCritic manifests as thought patterns associated with imposter syndrome. These can include:

People can see through me.
I'm a fraud.
What makes me think I am qualified for this role?
I don't know how to complete this process from start to finish, so I shouldn't even start.
Everyone has more experience than me.
I am not worthy.
Why did I think I could do this?
I need someone else to encourage me or structure me.
I should just wait until I feel more confident and capable.

Your InnerCritic thrives on perfectionism, making it hard to feel worthy of success or acceptance. Your personality type and upbringing are strongly associated with developing these imposter thought patterns. For example, if you were raised in an environment that celebrated achievement over effort and associated self-worth with winning, you are more likely to seek this external validation as you age, constantly battling your InnerCritic's idea of success.

As we enter adulthood, many of the concrete and objective structures for achievement fade. Those who are raised in households that prize and celebrate academic achievement often experience a quarter-life crisis in their early twenties when these success milestones become much less frequent. Friendships change, academic frameworks disappear, grades are no longer given, and extracurricular activities are not easily accessible. With this change, the InnerCritic becomes louder, challenging our ability to create new structures and find new sources of validation. The InnerCritic often overlooks the importance of nurtured relationships, mental and physical health, and lifestyle, preferring tangible honors, awards, and merits.

Tips on How to Rewire Your Thinking

- When someone acknowledges you or gives you a compliment, simply reply with a "thank you." Resist the urge to let your InnerCritic downplay your efforts by responding with, "Thanks, but it was just luck." This may feel awkward at first, but over time, you will break the habit of letting your InnerCritic diminish your achievements.
- Be mindful of how and why you share information about yourself. Avoid passive statements intended to withdraw validation from others. For example, saying, "I don't really deserve this recognition; others worked harder" minimizes your accomplishments and invites others to question your worth. The value of these emotional deposits is fleeting and only temporarily appeases your InnerCritic. This void will only begin to fill when you commit to believing in yourself and adopting a lifestyle that embraces the process of success rather than the perfection your InnerCritic demands.
- Friendly competition can be empowering, but operating primarily through a competitive lens creates intense pressure and can fuel your InnerCritic's narrative of your own inferiority. Surround yourself with people who can openly celebrate growth and collaboration.
- Words matter. Practice sharing statements that begin with, "I am proud of my efforts in . . ." or "It has been really satisfying to . . ." This speech framework encourages internal validation and helps counter the negative self-talk of your InnerCritic. Remember, statements like these are not bragging—they are a way to acknowledge your efforts and keep your InnerCritic in check.

- Avoid comparing yourself to others. Now more than ever we are exposed to curated snapshots of others' lives, which can trigger a strong comparison mindset. Success is not a concrete destination but a process, one that your InnerCritic often oversimplifies. Also, we all know that social media is a curated look at the best moments people choose to share, not a genuine reflection of someone's lived life. Recognize that others' achievements are part of their journey and should not be seen as threats but as separate experiences that do not diminish your own.
- Start by redefining what success means to you. Think of it as a process rather than a defining moment. Success is a journey, one that requires vulnerability, internal validation, and realistic expectations—traits that can help silence your InnerCritic. When asked about your greatest success, try responding with a statement that acknowledges the ongoing journey, such as, "I'm still on my journey. I am proud of my achievements along the way, but it's the setbacks that have really encouraged the most growth."

Check-in Questions

To me, success means . . .

When do I feel most successful?

Who do I consider successful, and what qualities or achievements lead me to this categorization?

What setbacks have shaped my understanding of success?

Does success look different in various areas of my life? If so, how?

What unrealistic expectations do I hold about success, and how can I challenge them?

How do I typically respond to the success of others?

Over the years, I have worked with many clients who struggle with the thinking patterns and anxieties associated with imposter syndrome. Their InnerCritics are usually fierce and encourage constant battles with self-doubt and the fear of failure. These individuals, whether elite athletes or CEOs, typically set high standards for themselves, influenced by their InnerCritic's notion of success. While they may appear confident, they are often deeply affected by the negative self-talk that the InnerCritic perpetuates.

Those with a loud InnerCritic rise to the occasion when faced with challenges or critical feedback, driven by the innate need to prove themselves. This drive frequently leads to anxiety and insecurity as their InnerCritic forgets past successes and continuously questions their worth and abilities. This cycle heightens their sensitivity to others' opinions and nonverbal cues, resulting in negative and damaging narratives. This is especially true for serial fixers, who carry the additional burden of resolving issues for others. One method I teach my clients to quiet the InnerCritic is to pause and seek more information before making assumptions, as what we assume about the unknown is usually negative. Instead, assess whether it is appropriate to ask questions or wait for information to come to you. Those suffering from imposter syndrome often operate with a sense of urgency, feeling the need to control the unpredictable, which leads to impulsive decisions that ultimately sabotage rather than remedy.

By recognizing and challenging your InnerCritic's voice, you can begin to open a mindset that embraces vulnerability, internal validation, and realistic expectations. People are not thinking about you as much as your InnerCritic would have you believe. Embrace the process and allow yourself to grow through life's journey, with all its risks, tumbles, and triumphs. Expectations can be a double-edged sword. Some may suggest avoiding expectations to prevent disappointment, while others argue they are necessary to stay focused. It's crucial to distinguish between expectations for people and expectations for objects or processes. For instance, expecting your child to be cheerful every morning can set you up for conflict, as they will naturally have days when cheer just isn't possible.

We must extend this same courtesy to ourselves. The InnerCritic amplifies the gap between our expectations and reality, thriving on rigidity and insisting we should have done more or been better. Life's unpredictability requires that we adjust our expectations accordingly. For serial fixers, this can be particularly challenging. Even when you follow the same daily routine, no two days are exactly the same. The InnerCritic ignores these nuances, however. It wants the same high, measurable output from you, regardless of what hurdles you encounter.

If you constantly feel disappointment, try changing your mindset toward acknowledging the many factors which exist beyond your control. This isn't about adopting passivity, but rather appreciating that the world is complex and ever changing, and people or places are not responsible for making you feel a certain way.

The InnerCritic may try to convince you that if you do more, push harder, or be better, you can avoid disappointment. But the truth is, disappointment is a part of life, and no amount of self-criticism will change that. Be proactive and give yourself grace. If you create expectations for yourself, factor in your current circumstances and the cards life dealt you. Defuse the InnerCritic by acknowledging that the goal is progress, not perfection.

Meet Jason

Jason, a serial fixer, had fallen behind academically, and his perpetual drive to fix everything for everyone else had taken a toll on him. He couldn't seem to muster the motivation to complete his assignments and often found his attention wandering during class. His mind was clouded with anxious thoughts, constantly churning with the burdens of those he felt responsible for. Logically, he understood that no one else could see the rapid succession of worry pulsing through his mind and body. On the outside, he appeared cool, calm, and collected, but internally, he was battling relentless anxieties—primarily centered on his health—while constantly fending off his InnerCritic, which fed him a steady stream of potential negative judgments that he imagined others were entertaining.

Over the last year, Jason's **health anxiety** had spiked, fueled by his instinct as a serial fixer to solve everything in his life and the lives of those around him. Even basic routines like eating or sleeping became incredibly triggering. The basics were falling apart. He was up most nights. The sleep he did get was punctuated by fitful hours, leading to frequent school absences. His relationships with family members were strained by the neglect of his own needs. His hope for improvement was vanquished by his InnerCritic, which thrived in this chaos, amplifying his fears and intensifying the sense that he wasn't good enough for anything.

> **health anxiety**—Excessive worry and anxious thoughts about one's health. This condition often involves frequent research into health issues, which can exacerbate anxiety symptoms and lead to compulsive behaviors. Individuals may find it challenging to self-soothe and stay present with current information or facts, as their anxiety can overwhelm rational thinking.

In therapy, we began focusing on two initial areas: reestablishing structure around his basic needs and exploring the role of his InnerCritic—how it protected him but also intensified his anxiety. Like many teens, Jason was initially reluctant to open up, but he responded well to questions that validated his experiences and curiosity. Though he logically knew he wasn't the only person suffering from these symptoms, his InnerCritic made him feel isolated and unique. It convinced him that no one else had it quite as bad and trapped him in a cycle where he constantly attempted to fix himself and everyone else, preventing him from feeling whole and alive.

Exhaustion fueled his symptoms and kept him awake at night, while his InnerCritic berated him for not being able to "get it together." It was a vicious cycle—his energy levels and emotions dictated how he stumbled through life, forcing him into reactive, ill-prepared interactions. When these interactions went poorly, as they often did, his InnerCritic grew louder and scolded him for his failures, fueling anxiety and a sense of inadequacy.

Every time Jason entered my office, he had diagnosed himself with something new. He was desperate for an explanation to quiet his InnerCritic. If there was a reason for the shortcomings, he could debate back with his InnerCritic. He poured over research, trying to make sense of his symptoms and lack of control, just as he had attempted to fix the problems of those around him. Instead of dismissing or explaining away his anxiety, we began working on understanding it. We acknowledged that his InnerCritic, though harsh, was ultimately trying to protect him. We asked questions: What was this part of him trying to shield? What parts of Jason were being overshadowed by this constant self-criticism?

Getting curious about his inner critic and learning to appreciate its intentions helped defuse the internal conflict. Jason's all-or-nothing thinking, often driven by his InnerCritic, was a major source of his exhaustion. We learned that Jason's rigid self-judgments weren't the answer; they were part of the problem.

As sessions progressed, Jason gained more awareness and began to understand the importance of establishing a healthy structure—something he had to create and own. My role was to support and guide, but Jason needed to design a plan based on what he learned about himself—his tendencies, triggers, and the ways his inner critic drove him to exhaustion, not just in his life but in his attempts to fix everyone else's.

He started small, setting manageable boundaries, particularly around sleep, and recognized how his excessive screen time exacerbated his fatigue and impaired his ability to care for himself. His InnerCritic would tell him he was wasting time, but as Jason implemented structure and boundaries, he began to quiet that voice. He found that even small steps, like reducing screen time before bed, allowed him to regain some control.

The overarching theme in our work was creating a structure that allowed Jason to be proactive in his life rather than constantly reacting to crises—both real and imagined. His InnerCritic had always framed him as a victim, helpless in the face of life's demands, ultimately trying to shield him from limitations, ailments, injuries, or illnesses. This was all in an effort to support his motto: to live every day to the fullest. Reframing his thought patterns—learning to challenge this narrative—helped Jason recognize his own power and agency, not just in fixing himself but also in how he approached others.

Patience, grace, and self-awareness became essential tools in this process. Jason learned to collect data about himself rather than judge his every move. He began to see himself as a work in progress rather than a failure, a shift that slowly quieted the InnerCritic's harsh assessments. He identified his **nonnegotiables**—what he needed to do daily to feel stable—and reframed the InnerCritic's harsh demands into more supportive, goal-oriented thoughts.

> **nonnegotiable**—An essential practice or activity that a person consistently prioritizes as part of their self-care routine, such as a morning workout or quiet time. Nonnegotiables are critical to their well-being and protected in their schedule.

As Jason embraced this new structure, a fresh appreciation for his anxiety emerged.

Rather than scrambling for answers, he began to check in with himself, learning to make sense of his urges, triggers, and soothing practices. His InnerCritic, once a dominant voice, shifted to the back seat as Jason built self-trust. Once he understood what role this aspect played, it no longer had both hands on the wheel. By learning to prioritize his own needs, Jason began to shift from a serial fixer of others to a more balanced caretaker of himself.

Meet Catherine

Catherine, a seasoned HR professional in her mid-forties, had long been the backbone of her organization, admired for her dedication and tireless work ethic. However, as her responsibilities grew, she began to grapple with an overwhelming sense of burnout that seeped into every aspect of her life. The demands of her role became heavier, compounded by the impossibly high expectations she placed on herself. Known as the go-to person for her team, Catherine was always ready to lend a hand or provide support, but this unrelenting drive came at a significant personal cost.

Her InnerCritic played a central role in this struggle, constantly reminding her of the high standards she had set for herself. "You should be doing more," it whispered, unyielding and harsh. It magnified her perceived shortcomings and overshadowed her successes, making even her accomplishments feel hollow. During our sessions, Catherine often shared how this relentless self-judgment eroded her mental and emotional well-being. "I can never seem to do enough," she admitted, her eyes reflecting a mix of frustration and exhaustion. Each day felt like a battle against her own mind, leaving her drained by the time she returned home.

Adding to her stress, Catherine was deeply frustrated by the disengagement and overwhelmed feeling she noticed in her staff. Despite her efforts to create a positive workplace culture, morale was low, and many team members seemed unmotivated. "It's like I'm failing them," she said, her voice heavy with disappointment. She internalized her team's struggles, believing that their challenges were a direct reflection of her abilities as a leader. "If they're struggling, it means I'm failing as a leader," she often repeated, reinforcing the idea that her worth was tied to their well-being.

This relentless self-criticism only deepened her burnout, creating a vicious cycle. Catherine's desire to support her team turned into a sense of obligation, driving her to take on more than she could handle. "I feel like I have to solve every problem," she confessed, her weariness evident. "But I can't keep doing this without taking a step back." This realization marked a turning point as she began to recognize the toll her mindset was taking on her health and happiness.

Her InnerCritic also cast a long shadow over her personal life. Whenever she tried to carve out time for herself—whether for a walk or a quiet evening with a book—guilt would flood in, telling her she was neglecting her team or family. "How can I justify taking a break when everyone else is working so hard?" she wondered, grappling with the deeply ingrained belief that self-care was a luxury she couldn't afford. This guilt further drained her, as she continuously neglected her own needs in a futile attempt to meet the demands of those around her.

In our sessions, we worked on strategies to address her InnerCritic, with self-compassion becoming a cornerstone of our approach. Together, we explored the critical voice that had long dictated her choices and actions. Through exercises designed to foster self-kindness, Catherine began to glimpse an alternative narrative. "What if I treated myself with the same compassion I offer others?" she asked, opening the door to the possibility that prioritizing her well-being could coexist with her commitment to her team.

Learning to set healthy boundaries was another crucial aspect of her journey. Initially, this was a challenge. Catherine's nurturing instincts often clashed with her need for personal space. "It feels wrong to say no," she admitted, visibly torn. But as we reframed her understanding of boundaries, she began to see them not as selfish but as essential for sustainable leadership. She realized that taking care of herself enabled her to lead more effectively, rather than detracting from her role.

This process required practice and experimentation. Catherine worked to reassure both her nurturing and critical parts that she could still access her resilience and drive while allowing herself moments to pause and recharge. She started by scheduling short breaks throughout her day and delegating tasks to her team. These small steps began to replenish her energy, enabling her to be a more present and engaged leader.

Over time, Catherine developed a healthier internal ecosystem, fostering a more balanced and supportive relationship with herself. Instead of viewing her InnerCritic as an adversary, she learned to engage with it compassionately. "I can hear you, but I don't have to listen," she reminded herself during moments of doubt. This shift in perspective was empowering, allowing her to reclaim her narrative and embrace self-care without guilt or shame.

As she implemented these strategies, Catherine started noticing positive changes—not just in her own well-being but in her team's dynamics. With her newfound balance, she became more attuned to her staff's needs and emotions, creating an environment where they felt safe to express their struggles. "I think I'm finally starting to create the culture I've always wanted," she reflected one day, pride evident in her voice.

Catherine's story serves as a powerful reminder of the importance of self-care and the profound impact of our inner dialogue on overall well-being. By addressing her InnerCritic, she not only overcame burnout but also emerged as a more empathetic and effective leader. Her growth illustrates how transforming our relationship with ourselves can ripple out to improve our professional and personal lives.

Aligning with Our Inner Parts

By recognizing and aligning with their inner parts, individuals can navigate their personal and professional worlds more effectively. This awareness sheds light on how these various parts—the InnerCritic, the InnerRescuer, and the InnerPleaser—shape our thoughts, emotions, and behaviors, often influenced by our past experiences.

When we acknowledge these different parts, we can begin to disentangle their messages from our true desires and needs. For instance, while the InnerCritic may drive us to excel, its overwhelming influence can lead to burnout. Conversely, the rescuing part encourages self-care but can also instill guilt if we feel we're neglecting our responsibilities. By recognizing these conflicting messages, we can cultivate a compassionate internal dialogue, fostering deeper self-acceptance and healthier relationships.

Once we gain insight into ourselves and the roles our parts play, we can align with them and set boundaries. This alignment isn't about silencing any single part; rather, it's about harmonizing them into a cohesive internal ecosystem, as emphasized by the IFS model. Engaging with each part allows us to negotiate the InnerCritic's harshness while empowering our nurturing side to offer support without guilt.

Setting boundaries becomes an act of self-respect and care. It helps us define what is acceptable, creating space for our needs and allowing us to show up authentically. When our inner parts are aligned, we can tackle challenges with resilience and a greater sense of control. The work involved in soothing our inner parts is ongoing, requiring patience and a commitment to self-discovery. Yet the rewards are profound: a life marked by fulfillment, healthier relationships, and enhanced well-being. Embracing our inner parts enriches our lives and lays the groundwork for the fundamental work of establishing boundaries in chapter 4.

Part 2

Become a Space Creator

Imagine creating spaces where needs, values, and respect are prioritized, where relationships are healthy, and where clarity and presence are accessible. A "space creator" aims to achieve this not only for others but also for themselves. Being a space creator is more than just holding boundaries; it is about mindfully living, not merely surviving in cramped emotional quarters. While this may seem far-fetched, becoming a space creator is achievable and within reach, though it may require some reshuffling and reprioritizing.

Space creators practice a sustainable way to be present for others, offering them a place where they feel seen and heard without shouldering their burdens or replicating the tendencies of a serial fixer. When you do this well, you can leave conversations and interactions feeling unburdened, not weighed down by what happens in their lives. This is the essence of "Support, Don't Solve," that is, offering support while allowing others to own their experiences and choices rather than taking false ownership or responsibility.

Once you understand how to create space for others, you will begin to see how crucial it is to apply this practice to yourself.

In the following chapters, you will deepen your self-awareness and discover practical frameworks and tools to experiment with right away. With a strong emphasis on strengthening self-trust and building emotional resilience, you will acquire the skills to respond to life with confidence, maintain your boundaries, and apply the art of presence. Becoming a space creator is not just about making room in your life; it is about designing it with the intention to empower both yourself and those around you.

Chapter 4

Boundaries, Let's Start with You

Many of my consulting clients are leaders in the nonprofit sector, and the levels of empathy and determination that these individuals demonstrate are nothing short of exceptional. They are driven by a profound mission to serve others, helping those they assist navigate significant obstacles in their pursuit of basic needs and the next steps toward enhancing their overall quality of life. I have also observed that these leaders often contend with a fierce InnerCritic and a strong desire to please others. While they certainly understand the principles of self-care—frequently emphasizing its importance to those they support and love—they struggle to apply this wisdom in their own lives. It's one thing to advocate for others to establish boundaries and prioritize their well-being, but when these leaders attempt to do the same, they risk losing their focus. They may fear being perceived, by both themselves and others, as uncaring, selfish, or neglectful of their commitments to the greater good. The pressure can become immense.

Like many individuals in the "helping professions," they find themselves anchored to the challenges and hardships of others, using these as both a source of structure and a sense of purpose in life. They create space and framework for others to gain momentum and clarity, which is truly admirable. However, when this energy is predominantly directed outward, leaving little reserved for personal reflection and growth, it can compromise self-trust, lead to exhaustion, and risk a disconnect from their own inner selves. Engaging in internal work and self-reflection is undoubtedly difficult and many find it more rewarding to seek external sources for structure rather than using their own inner landscape as the primary arena for growth.

A boundary is something put in place to provide security, predictability, or safety. It is an attempt to reduce triggering events or situations that create chaos within your internal ecosystem. Healthy boundaries stem from self-awareness, pattern recognition, and ongoing maintenance. Maintenance is crucial in this context; it involves regularly checking in with your values and recognizing your impulses or go-to methods of distraction—those attempts to self-soothe or prevent certain feelings or parts of yourself from surfacing. Ongoing maintenance helps ensure that your boundaries remain effective and aligned with your evolving needs.

Creating and sustaining internal boundaries is a challenging task, especially for serial fixers who often prioritize the needs of others over their own. This pattern can make it difficult to assert personal limits, as they may feel guilty or anxious about disappointing others. Many serial fixers were not shown healthy boundary-setting behaviors early in life, leading them to rely on external cues for guidance rather than trusting themselves. This struggle is compounded by the fear that setting boundaries might alienate those they care about or expose their vulnerabilities.

For people who struggle with boundaries, their Inner-Pleaser becomes the primary driver in decision-making and relationships. These people often try to avoid conflict, avoid disappointing others, and chase the label of a good person in all their interactions. As they encounter painful, confusing, or fear-inducing experiences, their InnerCritics become more prominent. Their boundaries vary, swinging from loose and nonexistent to overly rigid, which can perpetuate feelings of isolation and hinder their ability to truly know themselves or others beyond a superficial level. Engaging with anything deeper can feel overwhelmingly intense and perilous. They haven't given themselves the time or space to prepare or take steps to avoid discomfort or others' judgments, which reflects a lack of self-trust. They believe that the experiences they've gathered throughout their lives are invalid, leading them to doubt their resilience and resourcefulness when unexpected disruptions arise.

For many clients I've worked with, anxiety drives their challenges with boundaries. This anxiety is rooted in deeper fears, reflecting the motivators behind their boundary issues. While it can be exhausting, anxiety plays a key role in keeping them from being fully present, as it often focuses on anticipating future threats or revisiting past events. For those with loose or rigid boundaries, anxiety can further undermine their ability to maintain authentic connections or trust themselves, leading to an internal struggle for control and stability.

Sometimes, the boundaries you set for yourself can feel logical, yet they may be challenged by internal parts of you with conflicting motivations. These parts, driven by a desire to protect your peace or avoid missing out, might resist those boundaries. Craving freedom or spontaneity, they can push you to reconnect with overlooked or dormant aspects of yourself, sometimes bulldozing through the very boundaries you've set. Before you can successfully integrate a healthy boundary, preliminary work is necessary. This involves self-awareness—checking in with yourself, collecting data, and understanding what drives certain behaviors and thought patterns. What are the motivators? What are these parts of you trying to protect or prevent? In the next chapter, you will learn practical self-awareness techniques to help you gather data, build self-trust, and begin to align and appreciate all (yes, all) of your parts.

Types of Boundaries

There is more than one kind of boundary. Some boundaries monitor and regulate aspects of your life, such as time, energy, space, health, and relationships. If your InnerPleaser or InnerCritic has taken up excessive real estate within you and often runs the show, you might establish strict boundaries around what you disclose or what roles you play with others. Conversely, your boundaries could be vague, allowing others to dictate where you fit in and how much you contribute. In either case, it's important to begin understanding what these parts of yourself are trying to achieve or protect you from.

Temporal boundaries involve setting limits on how you spend your time and who gets to share it. These boundaries ensure that your time is respected and that you have enough for rest, self-care, and personal priorities. For instance, if work tasks are creeping into your evenings and weekends, you might decide to establish specific work hours and refrain from checking emails after a certain time.

Emotional boundaries protect your emotional well-being by making sure your feelings and needs are acknowledged and respected. They prevent others from overwhelming you with their emotions or expecting you to take responsibility for their feelings. Imagine a friend who frequently vents about their problems without considering your emotional capacity; an emotional boundary might involve gently letting them know that while you care, you can only listen for a limited time before needing a break.

Physical boundaries refer to your personal space and physical touch, helping you feel safe and comfortable in your body and environment. If someone invades your personal space or touches you without consent, it's essential to express your need for space or ask them to refrain from physical contact.

Mental boundaries protect your thoughts, beliefs, and opinions. They give you the right to your own ideas without being pressured into thinking a certain way by others. For example, if someone is trying to impose their views on you, you might politely state that you respect their opinion but prefer to maintain your own perspective.

Material boundaries involve setting limits on how you share or protect your possessions, finances, and resources, ensuring that your material needs are met and that you aren't taken advantage of. For example, if a family member frequently borrows money without repaying it, you might decide to set a limit on how much you're willing to lend or choose not to lend money at all.

Relational boundaries define the roles you play in relationships and help ensure they are balanced and mutually respectful. These boundaries prevent codependency and allow for healthy connections. If you often find yourself taking on the role of caregiver in a relationship, it may be time to communicate your needs and ask for more reciprocal support.

Energy boundaries are about managing where you invest your energy, making sure you have enough left for yourself. These boundaries help prevent burnout and maintain your well-being. For instance, if social interactions leave you feeling drained, you might limit the number of social events you attend each week or schedule downtime afterward to recharge.

Cultural and Familial Influences on Boundaries

The formation of boundaries is often deeply influenced by cultural and familial backgrounds. Some cultures emphasize collectivism, which can make it more challenging for individuals to establish personal boundaries. The needs of the group may be prioritized over the individual, leading to a tendency to sacrifice personal boundaries for the sake of harmony. Strong feelings of guilt can impact a person's ability to set certain boundaries, grant themselves permission to feel a certain way, or improve their relationship with themselves. Conversely, in cultures that prioritize individualism, boundaries may become too rigid, creating a sense of isolation and disconnection from others. Underestimating your energy levels and ability to adapt or rally in certain situations or with certain individuals begins to feel confining. This setup usually results in loneliness and intense internal battles that intensify a victim-driven mindset or filter. Understanding these cultural influences can provide insight into why you may struggle with setting boundaries and how to navigate these challenges in a way that honors both your heritage and your personal needs.

Practical Strategies for Establishing Boundaries

Creating boundaries involves more than just identifying what you need; it also requires knowing how to implement and maintain them effectively. Begin by recognizing patterns in your behavior and emotions. Journaling can be a valuable tool in this process, helping you track situations where your boundaries were tested or where you felt uncomfortable or overwhelmed. Reflect on these moments and consider what boundary might have helped you navigate the situation more effectively.

Understanding your limits and capacities is essential. If your plate often becomes too full, leaving you perpetually exhausted or resentful, it may be a sign that you are neglecting your needs. This might indicate that you allow others' needs to dictate your daily schedule and energy levels. Be mindful if your InnerPleaser is influencing your decision. Are you saying yes just to avoid disappointing someone or to dodge the discomfort of setting a boundary?

To help you decide whether to say yes, try using the three reasons test. This simple exercise ensures your yes is intentional and aligned with what truly matters to you. Identify at least three compelling reasons before agreeing to something, such as

passion for the activity: You might say yes because it aligns with your commitment to a cause you care about. For instance, volunteering at a local school can reflect your passion for education.

opportunity for growth: Agreeing to something can provide a chance to learn new skills, such as taking on a leadership role in a group project, which can boost your confidence and experience.

supporting a friend: You may want to say yes because you feel a desire to reciprocate past support. If a friend helped you during a tough time, you might feel compelled to lend a hand when they ask for assistance.

Setting boundaries is a vital form of self-care, but when used as a shield or an excuse, they can become counterproductive. Maintaining meaningful relationships often involves sacrifice, empathy, and compromise. Boundaries are not just about meeting your own needs; they also require balancing those needs with the needs of others. Healthy boundaries within relationships are built on mutual respect and understanding. Being attuned to yourself allows you to navigate interactions authentically, recognizing when to push and when to set limits effectively.

Introducing a new boundary or saying no can be intimidating. Use "I" statements to take ownership of your feelings, which helps reduce defensiveness and prevents others from internalizing your request as a personal failure. Fear of damaging relationships or altering someone's perception may prevent you from communicating your needs effectively. Owning your decision to participate or decline can help you remain present and enjoy life more fully.

Saying no is challenging but necessary in some cases. Authentically subscribing to your "no" takes self-reflection and check-ins. What are your true motivators—internally, who's running the show? Are there other parts of you that need to have a voice? What are you trying to avoid by going with the flow or presenting as available even though you're not?

- Be clear and respectful when saying no. Avoid over-explaining, which can heighten anxieties and create confusion about your message.
- Understand that this practice can be uncomfortable and requires practice to improve. It's all about reps! The first step is to check in with yourself and recognize tendencies that lead to stress and overcommitment.
- Acknowledge your current situation, goals, and limits. During significant life changes or hardships, it's essential to honor your need for focus and avoid over compromising.
- Prioritize your values and goals. Setting boundaries around these nonnegotiables is vital for maintaining trust with yourself and supporting your mental health.
- Listen to your intuition and don't let your Inner-Pleaser take over. Those warning signals are important. Ignoring them to please others often leads to more significant issues later.
- Set boundaries early and avoid last-minute cancellations, which can strain relationships and indicate that you are pushing your limits.
- Seek support from friends, family, or a trusted confidant. Sharing your thoughts can provide a fresh perspective and alleviate feelings of guilt.
- Shift your mindset from guilt to self-care or empowerment. Reflect on your experiences and use them as tools for growth, helping you avoid repeating past patterns.

- Communicate clearly and challenge irrational thoughts that contribute to guilt. Assess whether your guilt is based on realistic concerns or unfounded fears, and understand what your InnerCritic is trying to protect.

Navigating the balance of saying no and establishing healthy limits is not about closing doors but about opening yourself to more authentic connections and experiences. If you find yourself consistently saying yes to requests that drain your energy, it might be time to set a boundary around your availability. Establish specific times for helping others while ensuring you have adequate time to recharge. Setting boundaries is not about excluding others but creating a space where you can engage with the world sustainably and in alignment with your values. It's about finding a flow that works for you and adjusting it as you progress through different chapters of life and pursue new goals.

While boundaries are essential for maintaining well-being, they can bring unexpected emotional challenges, including feelings of grief. Setting a boundary doesn't guarantee that others will follow it, and when boundaries aren't respected, it can lead to painful shifts in relationships, causing you to mourn the loss of familiar dynamics. In these moments, you may face a difficult choice: to adapt to the changed relationship or to stand firm, even if it means letting go of something you once cherished.

Boundaries are deeply personal and don't require others' validation to be legitimate. Consistently reinforcing them can help others gradually understand and respect them, even if they don't see their necessity. At times, however, you may choose not to communicate a boundary if it feels unsafe or if you doubt the other person's respect for your limits. These boundaries are set silently, which can lead to inner conflict and grief over what might have been.

Ultimately, boundaries are about understanding what you can control—your own actions and reactions—while recognizing that you can't control others. Accepting this truth allows you to prioritize your well-being without expecting compliance from others or holding onto unrealistic hopes.

The Ongoing Process of Boundary Maintenance

Once boundaries are set, the work isn't over. You'll need to maintain and adjust your boundaries as life evolves. As you encounter new challenges, such as a demanding job or a significant relationship, it's important to reassess your boundaries to ensure they still serve you well. Life changes, and so should your boundaries. Regular check-ins with yourself can help you stay attuned to your needs and make the necessary adjustments to maintain balance and well-being.

Bodyguards

We might think about misaligned boundaries as metaphorical bodyguards. When you encounter a new experience, your mind begins to rifle through all of the things that could go wrong, how you might be left feeling abandoned, embarrassed, or depleted—all feelings you have felt before and since then have tried to avoid. And so, a handful of bodyguards appear in your mind's eye. Your mind and body make significant attempts to protect you, but they can come on too strong, leaving you feeling paralyzed and preventing you from channeling your more adventurous side that loves to take risks in order to learn and grow. In your past, risks may have resulted in negative consequences or forced you to navigate difficult, overbearing emotions, leading you to avoid them in the future. These experiences summon your bodyguards, and they create a fortress bounding you safely from experiences that may lead to these emotions again. I often reframe these situations with clients by sharing, "Wow, it looks like your mind provided you with ten bodyguards when you really only needed one." Regardless, your bodyguards are now on full alert. Even though they aim to protect, they tend to sabotage and take over, leaving little space for other parts of you. But once you understand what's happening, you can use this intense reaction to build self-awareness. It's a protective mechanism that, while helpful in small doses, may need to be dialed back to allow space for growth and resilience.

The first step is to acknowledge and offer gratitude to your bodyguards rather than inserting judgment or frustration. This gratitude practice will clear some space to create a new internal boundary. By validating and appreciating your bodyguards you will decrease the likelihood of getting trapped in a negative thought cycle that includes shame. Rather than working against your bodyguards, acknowledge them and view this gratitude as a way of soothing them so that they can relax and perhaps stand down a bit so that other parts of you have a chance to surface and cultivate more balance as you make a decision or continue an interaction.

Bodyguard Check-in

What thoughts or feelings activate your internal bodyguards?

When do you notice your bodyguards becoming overly protective?

How might your bodyguards be preventing you from taking risks that could lead to growth?

What is one small step you can take to reassure your bodyguards while still allowing space for your confident self to emerge?

How can you show gratitude to your bodyguards for their protection while inviting them to relax a bit?

In 2018, I took a risk and broadened my professional role. My passion for working with clients individually was unwavering, but I needed more. Growing up playing on teams, I missed that unity, support, and accountability. Thus I began speaking and facilitating wellness workshops for human resource professionals, sales managers, leaders, health care providers, teachers, and nonprofit workers. As you can imagine, the demand for workshops focused on mental wellness, burnout prevention, and resilience training skyrocketed as the pandemic continued through 2020 and into 2021.

I identified a common thread among these professionals. They all had an intense desire to serve and help but were also depleted and exhausted. Many reported high levels of burnout and operated with weak or poorly defined boundaries. They were prone to taking false ownership of others' problems and emotions while simultaneously trying to navigate their own. Their lives were structured around the needs of others, causing their stress levels to soar and their bodyguards to be on high alert. The effort to debrief and detach from the difficult experiences shared by clients, combined with their attempts to soothe and fix those issues, disrupted their sleep and made it challenging to be present in their own lives. As a result, they found themselves trapped in an exhausting cycle, operating on autopilot and increasingly disconnected from their own needs and emotions. Many experienced compassion fatigue, prioritizing others over their well-being. Controlled by their InnerPleasers and InnerRescuers, these protective bodyguards hindered their overall well-being and balance, clearly reflecting the toll I had faced many times before.

Serial fixers often lose themselves in the needs of others, neglecting their own well-being. Recognizing this pattern is the first step toward reclaiming energy and establishing healthy boundaries. Saying no is not merely refusal; it's about making space for what truly matters. Setting boundaries is self-care, allowing you to engage with the world authentically while ensuring your well-being remains a priority. Ultimately, it's not just about protecting your energy; it's about enhancing your capacity to serve others in a way that aligns with your values and goals.

It's essential for serial fixers to understand that boundary maintenance is ongoing. Life continually presents new challenges, but by regularly checking in with yourself and adjusting your boundaries as needed, you can navigate these changes with grace and confidence. You can ensure that your needs are met while serving others.

Chapter 5

Building Self-Trust

In today's fast-paced and hypercompetitive world, the concept of self-trust frequently takes a back seat to the relentless pursuit of external validation and success. People find themselves caught in a constant cycle of striving for perfection, driven by the fear of judgment from others and the relentless pressure imposed on themselves. But at what cost?

Serial Fixers and Self-Trust

Serial fixers prioritize the needs of others so intensely that they lose touch with their own instincts and desires. This outward focus erodes self-trust over time, as they become increasingly reliant on external feedback and validation to guide their actions. The urge to help and the need to be seen as capable humans frequently overshadow their ability to tune in to their own inner voice, leaving them questioning their decisions and doubting whether they're doing enough to meet others' expectations. The constant pressure to "fix" everything for everyone else clouds their judgment, making it difficult to trust themselves to make choices that honor their own needs and boundaries.

Developing self-trust is not only essential but transformative for serial fixers. It allows them to reclaim ownership of their choices and recognize that their worth is not tied to how well they manage others' needs. By nurturing self-trust, they can pause, listen to their intuition, and resist the urge to automatically take on others' burdens. This shift enables them to engage with the world from a place of strength and authenticity, rather than out of obligation or fear of letting others down.

Self-Trust Check-in Exercise: Small Moments, Big Impact

Though it may seem simple, this exercise can help serial fixers strengthen their self-trust in everyday situations. The next time you're asked a question like "Where do you want to eat?" "Which color do you prefer?" or "What time do you want me to pick you up?" pause. Take a moment to reflect and truly consider your answer before responding.

Serial fixers are often quick to say things like, "Whatever works" or "You choose," defaulting to accommodate others. While these micro-instances may seem insignificant separately, collectively they represent missed opportunities for self-connection and advocacy. By taking the time to respond thoughtfully, you create space to tune in to your preferences and values. These small moments of choosing for yourself help you build the muscle of self-trust, one decision at a time. And the best part? Someone else is structuring the question for you! All you have to do is listen to yourself.

External pressure. One of the primary obstacles to self-trust stems from the external pressures people face in their daily lives. From an early age, they are conditioned to seek approval and validation from others—whether it's parents, teachers, peers, or society at large. They fear being perceived as incapable or lazy, so they push themselves to constantly perform, to meet or exceed expectations, lest they fall short and face the consequences of judgment and criticism. This all-or-nothing mentality leads to rigidity and greatly impacts how they talk to themselves. People can't seem to give themselves grace or praise because it feels so unnatural. And yet internal validation and providing space for themselves are necessary components of maintaining a healthy relationship with themselves.

This external pressure to conform to societal standards of success creates a pervasive sense of insecurity and self-doubt. People become hyperaware of how others perceive them, constantly seeking validation and approval to validate their worth. As a result, their sense of self becomes contingent upon the opinions and judgments of others, eroding their confidence and undermining their ability to trust themselves.

The InnerCritic's role. In addition to external pressures, your internal critic—that relentless voice of self-doubt and self-criticism—exacerbates the struggle of self-trust. Fueled by perfectionism and the constant need to prove yourself, this inner voice sets impossibly high standards and berates you mercilessly when you fall short. It tells you that you're not good enough, that you need to do more, be more, and achieve more in order to be worthy of love and acceptance. The internal critic operates on a never-ending loop of comparison and self-judgment, driving you to push harder, work longer, and sacrifice your well-being in pursuit of an unattainable ideal. Serial fixers become trapped in a cycle of self-sabotage, where no amount of external validation can quell the relentless demands of their InnerCritic.

Caught in the grip of external pressures and internal criticism, serial fixers cling to the promise of relaxation and enjoyment as a distant reward for ceaseless efforts. They tell themselves that once they've achieved their goals, met their deadlines, and proven themselves worthy in the eyes of others, then—and only then—can they allow themselves to relax and enjoy life. But the reality is that this elusive promise of relaxation is an illusion. Serial fixers rarely give themselves permission to truly unwind and savor the present moment, always looking ahead to the next challenge, the next hurdle to overcome. They may be engaging in some self-care, but they often multitask and miss out on the true benefits of these rejuvenating practices. They are out of practice when it comes to the concentration and patience needed to be present in their current environment. As a result, they find themselves trapped in a state of perpetual exhaustion, disconnected from themselves and others, resentful of the relentless demands they place on themselves.

Serial fixers often mistake not being productive with wasting time. They worry that if they slow down, someone else may get ahead. If only they could fill their time with more, they could achieve more. Sometimes their logic can overcome this thought pattern, but emotionally, it generates fear. The very fear that fuels their never-ending "push" to keep going.

The reframe. Reframing begins with shifting focus inward, tuning out the noise of external expectations and aligning with the relentless chatter of the InnerCritic. Rather than dismissing and suppressing this driver, you attempt to understand it. What is it trying to protect? What does it fear? How can it be soothed? Recognize that your worth is inherent and unchanging, not dependent on your achievements or the opinions of others. Easier said than done, I know, but this sentiment can serve as a daily reminder and reset. It's challenging to subscribe to a new or updated mindset. Consistency and deliberate time for self-reflection and awareness generate reps, and it's those very reps that result in habit and lasting change.

Cultivating self-trust also means practicing self-compassion and self-care, prioritizing your well-being and honoring your needs and boundaries. It means embracing imperfections and acknowledging that failure is not a reflection of your worth but an opportunity for growth and learning.

Most importantly, cultivating self-trust requires relinquishing the illusion of control and surrendering to the inherent uncertainty of life. It means embracing vulnerability and trusting in your ability to navigate whatever challenges may come your way, knowing that you have the resilience and strength to weather storms. Trust that if you honor your boundary and leave loose ends for another day, you will complete them. You will persevere; you will survive. Trust that you can deliver, and it doesn't necessarily need to be right now. Certain tasks or to-dos can wait while you attend to other roles, relationships, or tasks. These intrinsic boundaries are some of the most challenging to set, but they are also some of the most important ones, as they tend to generate space for fun, relaxation, peace, and connection.

Questions to Ask to Build Self-Trust

In what areas of my life do I struggle to trust myself, and what factors contribute to this?

In moments of uncertainty, how can I reassure myself of my resilience and inner strength?

What activities, practices, or reps can I incorporate to help me build my sense of trust in myself?

Increasing Self-Awareness

Before diving into actionable steps, it's imperative to cultivate self-awareness—the foundation upon which self-trust is built. Self-awareness involves tuning in to your thoughts, feelings, and behaviors without judgment, allowing you to understand yourself on a deeper level and recognize patterns that may be undermining your confidence and trust in yourself. You don't have to engage or solve these problems. Instead, self-awareness is about acknowledging where you are in any given moment and understanding how you are responding. It involves consciously choosing to exist in the here and now, rather than getting caught up in internal chatter or focusing on worries and thoughts rooted in the future or past.

Mindfulness practice. Dedicate time each day to mindfulness meditation or simply practicing present-moment awareness. Notice your thoughts, emotions, and bodily sensations without attaching judgment or trying to change them.

Journaling. Set aside time for reflective journaling, where you can freely express your thoughts and feelings without censoring yourself. Explore recurring themes or patterns in your journal entries to gain insight into your inner world.

Seek feedback. Actively solicit feedback from trusted friends, family members, or mentors about how you're perceived and how your actions impact others. Be open to constructive criticism as an opportunity for growth. Be mindful of defensiveness; make efforts to tame your ego and absorb helpful information.

Self-reflection. Take regular moments to pause and reflect on your experiences, both positive and negative. What lessons can you glean from past successes and failures? How can you apply these insights to future endeavors?

Actionable Steps for Cultivating Self-Trust

Align with your InnerCritic. Whenever your InnerCritic surfaces with self-doubt or self-criticism, challenge its validity. Ask yourself if these thoughts are based on facts or distorted perceptions. Practice self-compassion by offering yourself kindness and understanding. Omit the fear that these tactics will diminish or compete with your drive, dedication, and productivity.

Set realistic expectations. Identify unrealistic expectations you may be placing on yourself and adjust them to be more achievable and aligned with your values. Break larger goals into smaller, manageable tasks, celebrating progress along the way.

Practice assertiveness. Assert your boundaries and communicate your needs effectively with others. Learn to say no when necessary and prioritize activities that align with your values and goals.

Celebrate your achievements. Acknowledge and celebrate your accomplishments, no matter how small. Cultivate a mindset of gratitude for your strengths and successes, fostering a sense of self-confidence and worth.

Embrace failure as growth. Shift your perspective on failure from a reflection of your inadequacy to an opportunity for learning and growth. Recognize that setbacks are inevitable on the path to success and resilience is built through adversity.

Seek support. Surround yourself with a supportive network of friends, family, or professionals who uplift and encourage you. Share your struggles and vulnerabilities openly, knowing that you're not alone in your journey.

By increasing self-awareness and implementing these actionable steps, you can gradually cultivate a deeper sense of self-trust and resilience, empowering you to navigate life's challenges with confidence and authenticity. Building self-trust is a journey, not a destination—so be patient and compassionate with yourself along the way.

The thought of adding or removing a habit from your routine can be overwhelming. Does your mind have a tendency to create roadblocks or distractions? Perhaps it tries to subtly convince you that the efforts involved in making a change are too daunting or not worth it. You, like many, may take refuge behind the excuse that you don't have the necessary time to make an adjustment or add something new. There is a relentless pull to "be on" all the time—responding to messages, keeping up with social media, and staying perpetually busy. This constant engagement leads to burnout, anxiety, and a disconnect from yourself. To counteract this, cultivate the ability to be comfortable with just being, without the surrounding distractions.

Building Trust Within Yourself

Set aside specific times each day to unplug from digital devices. This can be during meals, before bed, or as part of your morning routine. Throughout the day, you are likely transitioning between different roles, activities, or tasks numerous times. These transitions offer perfect opportunities to pause, check in with yourself, and observe your surroundings. Notice how your current environment impacts you. The urge to constantly check your devices under the guise of productivity often sabotages these moments to connect with yourself, those around you, or your immediate situation. Instead, use this time to engage in activities that don't involve screens, fostering a deeper connection with yourself and your environment.

Being alone doesn't have to mean being lonely. Spend time with yourself doing something you enjoy, whether it's taking a walk, practicing a hobby, or simply sitting in silence. Many people fear being alone because it is when daunting thoughts or suppressed anxieties tend to surface. Initially, breaking the habit of pacifying yourself with distractions can flood the mind with uncomfortable thoughts and feelings. This often stems from a lack of self-trust in navigating these themes, and the energy expended in masking them perpetuates a feeling of inner disconnect. It may feel uncomfortable at first to rid yourself of distractions and simply be. However, your brain uses these opportunities to clear mental clutter, and it will continue to do so unless you proactively manage it. Embrace these moments as opportunities to reconnect with your inner self and build a stronger foundation of self-trust.

When you are changing things up or learning a new skill, it's natural to feel challenged and uncomfortable. Remember, you've faced this discomfort before in different contexts: learning to walk, reading, cultivating friendships, or starting new roles. These tasks were once challenging, yet with time and repetition, they became second nature. Accessing your grit and patience is a tricky balance, but it's essential for growth. Embrace the discomfort as a sign of progress and trust in your ability to adapt and overcome.

Developing trust within yourself is key to feeling comfortable in solitude. Trusting yourself means believing in your ability to handle your thoughts, emotions, and experiences without needing external validation or distraction. Here are some ways to cultivate self-trust:

Listen to your intuition: Pay attention to your gut feelings and inner voice. Trust that you know what's best for you and make decisions based on your inner guidance.

Honor your commitments: Follow through on promises you make to yourself, no matter how small. This builds confidence and trust in your ability to meet your own needs.

Acknowledge your strengths: Regularly remind yourself of your strengths and past accomplishments. This reinforces a positive self-image and trust in your capabilities.

Regular self-check-ins and mindfulness practices can significantly impact your mental and emotional well-being. By making these practices a part of your daily life, you can:

- Increase self-awareness and emotional intelligence.
- Reduce stress and anxiety levels.
- Enhance your ability to stay present and focused.
- Improve your overall mental health and resilience.

Strengthening the relationship with yourself is an ongoing process that requires dedication, patience, and consistent practice. By incorporating these advanced strategies into your daily routine, you not only cultivate a deeper sense of self-connection but also build resilience and inner strength. Much like caring for a garden, this journey demands patience, attention, and consistent effort. As you tend to the soil of your inner being, you plant seeds of self-awareness and self-trust and witness their growth, creating a rich inner landscape of authenticity. Each moment of solitude, each instance of resisting constant distraction nurtures these seeds, fostering resilience and inner growth.

Through mindful nurturing and compassionate self-care, you gradually accumulate a reservoir of self-trust—a belief in your capacity to navigate life's challenges with clarity and resilience. These practices transcend mere mindfulness; they're about gaining confidence in your ability to honor your needs and live authentically. By embracing this process and committing to your growth, you lay the foundation for a more grounded, fulfilling existence where self-awareness and self-trust are the cornerstones of a truly fulfilled life that you actively participate in.

Why We Fear Self-Discovery

An inevitable part of the process of building self-trust is confronting our pain through remembering difficult emotions and past experiences that were challenging, lonely, or confusing. If we've been suppressing these emotions, they'll continue to interrupt our thoughts and beg for attention. If silenced they don't go away. Instead, they wait patiently for their opportunity for gaining closure and being released. Truly being present with yourself requires you to validate these parts of yourself, but also to know how and when to set internal boundaries. Addressing every emotion that presents itself throughout the day is just as exhausting as suppressing your emotions. The key is to find a balance and to recognize that these parts are trying to protect. They too are on your team.

Intrusive thoughts, anger, aggression, or negativity can be scary or shocking. If repeatedly ignored and detested, they tend to come back even stronger or will wait patiently until there is an opportunity to get your attention in a big way. It is almost as if they have secretly hit the gym for months, bulking up and rigorously training, just waiting for the moment they can pop in and demonstrate their strength, making it very difficult for you to fend off their newly acquired muscles.

Rather than fearing these parts or giving them more power by allowing them to define the essence of who you are, the brain is designed to experience an array of feelings. Carving out time in your day to just be or to fully engage in one task only is a great starting point when trying to integrate presence into your day and boost self-awareness. For many, this comes in the form of moving their body. The shifts in heart rate, breath, and temperature are hard to ignore. And whether you're challenging yourself to push a bit harder, or checking in with yourself and deciding to pull back the effort, a physical practice is a reminder that you are here, and this is now. Many fixers tend to view workouts as a method to stay healthy, and as simply another to-do in the day. But maintaining the mind is just as important as the maintenance required for your body. When you build self-trust, you'll build up your capacity to be present with yourself without an agenda. Tapping into the here and now with the expectation to just be a participant and surrender takes consistency. That "muscle" or practice will only be strengthened with reps. Before you engage in any mindfulness practice, ground yourself by asking: Does this work for me? Am I able to be present and access myself as I move through this? Am I falling into a robotic state and viewing this as something to cross off and push through? If that's the case, I'm going to miss out on the benefits. But when you can be present, you'll begin to clear your clutter, address the parts of you that need attention, and tap into you.

Daily Fixes: Self-Awareness Builders for the Serial Fixer

Here's a concept: Picture a pair of bookends holding a number of books in place. While some may be added or removed, the bookends remain strong, fulfilling their purpose of keeping everything upright. This concept can be applied to your life, serving as a tool to prevent rigidity while encouraging a structure that includes check-ins and accountability.

Try this morning bookend: Identify a few manageable tasks or practices to engage with in the morning, focusing on presence rather than multitasking. If you love coffee, consider how to enjoy it mindfully, unplugging from devices and using this time for self-check-ins regarding your feelings and energy levels.

Try this evening bookend: As each day presents new challenges and joys, allocate time in the evening to process your experiences and validate your efforts. This practice can take the form of movement or journaling. Consider a simple gratitude exercise like "sweet, sour, and service." Your "sweet" could be a positive moment from the day, your "sour" might highlight a challenging experience, and your "service" could reflect on how you supported someone else or acknowledge those who supported you.

These bookends are your pillars—providing control and peace amid the chaos, encouraging proactive living while emphasizing reflection and rejuvenation.

Acknowledge the Work You've Done—Celebrate Your Wins!

It's essential to honor your efforts—whether from the past year, semester, or life chapter. Reflect on what you've achieved, the obstacles faced, and the resilience demonstrated. What words resonate with this phase of your life? How have you grown? What lessons have you learned? This check-in transcends mere reflection; it's an act of self-connection and validation, creating space for recovery and renewal. Taking time for introspection strengthens self-awareness, confidence, and trust as you transition into the next stage of your life.

Set Realistic Expectations

As you step into new routines, reconnect with loved ones, or embrace time alone, clarify your intentions. Assess the effort required and consider the motivations behind your expectations. Are boundaries needed to protect your emotional well-being? Can you let go of control for smoother interactions? Cultivating self-awareness enables mindful, intentional approaches to these transitions, allowing you to stay grounded and avoid situations that provoke anxiety.

Create a Framework for Relaxation, Not Idleness

Deliberately structuring relaxation periods is vital for recharging but can be challenging. The act of slowing down may feel uncomfortable as unresolved thoughts arise. If relaxing is tough, it may indicate you're "out of shape" from taking breaks. Moments of pause can serve as workouts for your well-being; with practice, they become more comfortable and allow you to reflect.

Too much idleness can lead to avoidance and negative self-talk. To combat this, reconnect with old friends, revive hobbies, take a break from technology, or immerse yourself in nature. Relaxation and productivity can coexist harmoniously when balanced intentionally. You can adapt and refine routines and boundaries that best serve you, incorporating moments of reflection and relaxation that keep you centered—without falling into an all-or-nothing mindset.

CHAPTER 6

Getting into Emotional Shape

Are You Emotionally Fit?

You may have picked up this book because you identify as a serial fixer and are looking for tools to break free of your fixer tendencies. That's one of my goals in this book, and my "Support, Don't Solve" framework in part 3 offers those tools. But I have a deeper goal for everyone reading this book—that you'll increase your overall emotional fitness. Someone who is emotionally fit can oscillate between accessing resilience, grit, awareness, and regulation. This level of fitness requires mindful consistency and attentiveness to how one speaks to themselves, as well as a commitment to self-reflection and care. These individuals are not free from distress; rather, they have acquired a high level of self-trust and the ability to access their resilience to recover and persevere. This adaptability allows them to navigate life's challenges with a sense of urgency when needed, while also maintaining the flexibility and space to process emotions as they arise—or to circle back to them if a boundary has been established to stay focused.

Emotional fitness fosters clear communication, boundary setting, and empathy. Emotionally fit people are less at risk for burnout or compassion fatigue because they listen to their bodies and minds, recalibrating when they receive signals that something is off. They actively engage with their experiences, taking the time to assess their feelings and adjust course as needed. They actively participate in their own journey, honoring all their parts and creating an internal homeostasis as they continue to navigate and be present in their day-to-day lives.

Meet Amara

On the surface, Amara's level of self-care was an A+. She had a healthy bedtime routine, prepared meals for the week on Sundays, exercised regularly, and acted reliably at work and in her partnership with her live-in boyfriend. She was checking all the boxes, yet she still felt "emotionally off," and anxiety was taking up more space in her life than she wanted to admit, even to herself. She was becoming a ticking time bomb.

In the past, Amara had been able to manage and control her feelings of anger. Growing up, anger was an unwelcome expression and judged harshly. She learned that the only side was the bright side and viewed anger as a symbol of not having it all together. Lately, though, Amara noticed that her emotions escalated quickly when something didn't go her way, even if it was minor. At work, she could manage to keep it together, but if her morning routine didn't go as planned or if the dogs' paws were muddy after their morning stroll, it would set her off. She would feel angry and frustrated, and then the judgment would settle in, especially if her partner (always cool and calm) just happened to be in the line of fire of these emotions.

Amara was confused why she couldn't seem to reap the benefits of her self-care efforts. She was active, but her connection with herself was rarely her only priority. Amara was often multitasking and chasing achievement, and it was rare for her to relax her sense of urgency.

I introduced the word *pause* to Amara. As simplistic as it may seem, the word serves as an effective reminder. One part of her acknowledged it and seemed interested, but her anxiety wouldn't dream of slowing down to engage in something that might throw her off or decrease her productivity. She was already creating space for self-care practices; how could she create more? This is a common misconception when it comes to pausing and self-care. Pausing requires data collection and leads to discovering ways to implement strategies or boundaries that support what you've observed based on your needs. Many of us falsely assume that it will take huge amounts of time to connect with ourselves, which can make self-care seem daunting. But we're missing what's already right in front of us.

Each day Amara encountered gaps and silences but filled them with distractions. These gaps or pauses could be the very opportunities that might soothe and create peace. Capitalizing on the short, interstitial space throughout the day increased her ability to be present and trust herself. This change began to soothe the parts of her fueled by anxiety, doubt, and urgency.

Amara longed for this type of shift to happen—one that would grant her the permission to experience and validate her anger rather than experiencing it instantaneously and then trying to make her way out of the familiar judgment spiral as she made desperate attempts to keep her cool and focus at work. Her goals were achievable; they just required her to soothe her perfectionistic parts and start small. This was going to be a process. She was getting intrinsically in shape and needed to get a new set of emotional reps in.

Amara began to view the numerous transitions in her day as opportunities to pause and collect data. Sometimes she'd simply access her senses and notice where she was and how she felt. Other times she paused to check in and identify what feelings she was experiencing. The most challenging part of this was to remove any judgment. This was merely an exercise to collect data and begin to identify any patterns. Positive shifts were happening, and Amara began to sleep through the night and feel refreshed. It was almost as if she were clearing her own clutter rather than just being at the mercy of her next "explosion."

When anger did surface, as it will for all of us from time to time, Amara began to label it, use her "I" statements, and understand that if she acknowledged and validated the feeling and discomfort, it would pass faster. Over time, she found herself returning to a more desirable mindset. Perfectionistic tendencies were still battling for space, and anxiety was not going to give up without a fight. It was a start, though, and with time Amara began to welcome the silence rather than fear it. She was getting better at pausing to just be. She was building resilience and getting emotionally in shape.

Are You a "Well" Being?

I'm fascinated at how certain phrases surface culturally and are then reworked when they start to get a bad rap. *Mental health* switched to *mental wellness* and now there's a push to simply say *well-being*. This seems to be an attempt to combat the stigmas associated with mental health and make it more inclusive and normalized. This shift is encouraging, but it also highlights how deeply ingrained stigmas around mental health still are. The question of "Are you a 'well' being?" can take on many definitions. In some form or fashion, I integrate this concept into every intake evaluation to explore the person's understanding of the phrase and assess where they feel they are at. A "well" being isn't just someone free of illness, but rather someone who experiences balance, resilience, and inner peace. It reflects a state of being that integrates mental, emotional, and physical health. What would it look like if you were at peace? What would have to happen, or not happen, for you to consider yourself a "well" being, healthy or stable?

Whether you can listen to the cues and warning signs of your body is a good indicator of your level of self-awareness and connection. If you aren't self-aware and connected, the parts of you that aim to protect can have a tendency to go overboard, leaving you feeling imbalanced, unproductive, disconnected, or out of control. Another sign is the steady urge to put something off or procrastinate in order to avoid discomfort, choosing instead to simply relax or tackle another task. This constant redirection or inability to find motivation tends to not only lead to negative self-talk but also generates confusion and leads you further astray from your goals or responsibilities.

An effective place to start is to understand what these parts of you are trying to protect you from. Are they protecting you from failure, loneliness, or a feeling that you're incapable? These cautious parts of you are useful and regardless of how you feel about them, they need to be viewed as your allies, not your enemies. Reframing your relationship with them, showing them gratitude, and working collaboratively with them is much more effective than making attempts to silence them. In order to become a "well" being, it is crucial to acknowledge and collaboratively work with the parts of yourself that tend to limit your progression and engage in self-sabotage. These parts, although seemingly counterproductive, are not inherently negative. They often arise as protective mechanisms that developed over time due to past experiences or conditioning. By recognizing their presence and understanding their underlying motivations, you can engage in a compassionate dialogue with these aspects of yourself.

Instead of dismissing or fighting against these limiting parts, approach them with curiosity and empathy. This approach allows us to uncover the root fears or beliefs that drive their behavior. Acknowledging their presence and actively seeking to understand them creates an opportunity for growth and transformation. Engaging in a collaborative process with these limiting parts involves treating them as allies rather than adversaries. It is essential to listen to their concerns and acknowledge the positive intentions behind their actions. This compassionate exploration allows you to gain valuable insights into the deep-seated patterns that hold you back.

By embracing a sense of understanding and unity with these parts, you can gradually introduce new perspectives and beliefs that align with your desires for personal growth. Becoming a "well" being is not about eradicating or suppressing parts of yourselves, but rather about integrating and working collaboratively with all aspects of your being. It is through this compassionate engagement that you can move toward a state of greater self-acceptance, resilience, and overall peace. To cultivate a state of well-being, it is important to identify your nonnegotiables and the activities or practices that contribute to your overall health and well-being. Nonnegotiables are the fundamental aspects of self-care that you prioritize and commit to, regardless of other obligations or external circumstances. They are the boundaries that you set and seek to maintain for yourself. When your nonnegotiables are not honored, you are more prone to burnout, exhaustion, and resentment.

Start by reflecting on what truly nourishes and supports you. Consider the activities, habits, and routines that leave you feeling physically energized, mentally clear, and emotionally balanced. These could include regular exercise, a balanced diet, quality sleep, meaningful social connections, mindfulness or meditation practices, engaging in hobbies or creative outlets, or spending time in nature.

Once you have identified your nonnegotiables, make a conscious effort to prioritize and integrate them into your daily or weekly routine. Set clear boundaries around these activities and treat them as essential self-care practices rather than optional indulgences. Recognize that investing time and energy into your well-being is not selfish but rather a necessary foundation for living a fulfilling life. It's also important to note that your nonnegotiables may evolve over time, and it's essential to regularly reassess and adjust them as needed. Each person's needs and circumstances are unique, so what works for someone else may not work for you. Pay attention to your body, mind, and soul, and listen to the signals they send. This self-awareness will help you identify what you truly need to maintain a healthy balance.

Different phases and roles in life call for varying energy levels. Effectively navigating these shifts helps you stay connected to yourself and avoid slipping into an all-or-nothing mindset. Your emotional well-being depends on your ability to prioritize and strike a careful balance between grace and accountability as you move through life's stages.

Self-compassion is critical, especially when you inevitably stray from your nonnegotiables. Life's unpredictability can make it difficult to maintain every desired practice. Embrace flexibility and adaptability, and always aim to return to your core self-care routines. Even small, consistent steps toward well-being can significantly enhance your overall health and happiness.

Stress vs. Anxiety

Stress often arises from identifiable external triggers. For instance, a looming deadline, losing your job while bills pile up, or coping with the loss of a loved one. When demands feel overwhelming, stress and a sense of being overburdened are common. Many of us juggle multiple roles throughout the day, watching our to-do lists grow with a sigh. We've linked productivity to a state of urgency, mistakenly believing that feeling stressed equates to being efficient. This mindset, unfortunately, has seeped into our approach to self-care and rejuvenation. We even take a sense of pride in responding to "How are you?" with "Oh, I've been so busy" or "Fine, but my to-do list is endless." We think this reflects our value and purpose. Yet when busyness becomes the norm, it signals an imbalance and a lifestyle driven by reactivity rather than honoring nonnegotiables and living with intention.

Stress is not regarded as a pleasant experience, but it's inevitable and the changes that take place in your body have extremely important purposes. The symptoms of stress are your body's built-in activation system designed to warn or protect you. It's easy to forget that our minds and bodies are on our team and truly want the best for us. Thankfully, we are no longer stressed by predators or need to run for our lives. The stress sensations we feel, such as the changes in our breath, temperature, and heart rate, are the same as those our ancestors felt when confronted with danger. Today, however, many of the stressors we face are fabricated or amplified by how we perceive and process modern challenges.

Anxiety is triggered by internal stimuli. It is a reaction and how we process (or don't process) stress, an experience, or an interaction. During this time, all of our internal "parts" reveal themselves and compete for the driver's seat. Unlike stress, anxiety tends to linger even after the concern has passed. Stress is like a cold. Anxiety is like allergies. Both can have similar symptoms, but after you fight off a cold, you are symptom free. Allergies, on the other hand, require constant monitoring. They can often be manageable but may flare up and become debilitating.

Combatting Burnout

Burnout was once a topic associated only with grind culture among adult professionals, especially those in historically intense and demanding fields that could leave you feeling drained. But in the era of smart devices, social media, and relentless academic and social pressures, children and teens have become the newest victims of burnout. In the past, young people were spared because they had so many opportunities to authentically connect with peers and their environments and had pressure-free spaces. "Being on" was necessary at certain times of the day but wasn't seen as a state that had to be constantly maintained.

Burnout refers to the disconnect and disengagement related to one's profession or academic responsibilities. Motivation is low and resentment continues to build. Tasks become overwhelming and the need for distraction intensifies. Basic needs are neglected, substance use increases, and the usual sources of connection and fun are not as desirable. Burnout can be prevented by implementing healthy boundaries, which I will discuss later. Compassion fatigue is similar, but is more likely to be experienced by those in roles that require high levels of empathy and (you guessed it) compassion. Occupying a role that includes the emotions of others can be incredibly rewarding but leads to exhaustion and symptoms related to anxiety if certain practices aimed to reset and rejuvenate are not consistently practiced. Teachers for example tend to feel a connection with others when they help and educate. Their passion for nurturing others as they develop and persevere is again a way to connect and feel purposeful.

Ways to Prevent Burnout

Accept that change is part of life. Embracing change can be tough, especially since we often crave control, but the reality is that control is limited. Change is inevitable, and our response to it matters greatly. Instead of seeing change as a derailment or setback, try reframing it as a challenge, an obstacle, or even an opportunity. This shift in perspective can foster strength and optimism, aiding your recovery as a serial fixer.

Acknowledge what you have already accomplished and navigated. Just pause for a moment and think about all of the events, experiences, and conversations you have been involved in. They are over, in the past. You survived them, pushed through. Sometimes with grace and vigor and sometimes with pure luck. It is so important to encourage ourselves, our children, and our coworkers to take positive risks and welcome the unpredictable and uncomfortable. This is what builds resilience and creates memories to access later. The wins, the tears, the laughs, and the struggles—they all count. They are all part of your story. You are the creator and therefore have the power to ignite and utilize the strength and knowledge acquired from your past.

Maintain presence and perspective. Limit your distractions or at least identify what you're trying to escape from. A good rule of thumb is to avoid multitasking when interacting with others. If you can't be present, honor both yourself and the other person by scheduling a more appropriate time to connect. Attention spans are dwindling, and to cultivate deeper connections, we must engage fully with those in front of us, seizing opportunities for both small talk and meaningful conversations. The world isn't out to get you. Often we create our own chaos. Practice being a participant, recognizing that every situation offers a choice in how you respond or react. We are all interconnected; our words and actions matter and can impact others, sometimes more than we realize.

Challenge your mind and body: Keep learning and sweating! Never stop learning and connecting to your environment. Our bodies and our minds want us to thrive and be as healthy as we possibly can. They are on our team, not working against us. Our bodies and minds need to be nourished, challenged, replenished. View anxiety, pain, restlessness, or exhaustion as opportunities to set a boundary or invite something new into your world. They are signals to make adjustments or adapt a viewpoint or behavior.

Build a positive support network. Life will repeatedly force you to step back socially and reevaluate the types of relationships and exchanges you engage in. What role do you typically play in your relationships? Are you constantly seeking validation from others, or do you feel reenergized by your interactions? Strive to surround yourself with active listeners and cultivate relationships that are balanced and noncompetitive.

Complete small tasks from start to finish. Whether you create daily checklists or schedule reminders to keep yourself focused, recognize the power of the process. We build momentum and confidence every time we start something and see it through to completion. This could be as simple as making your bed or washing your face. These basic routines demonstrate respect for yourself and your environment. The focus and the control required to finish something creates purpose and builds resilience. Perhaps try something completely new like learning another language, listening to a genre of music, or cooking a dish from a different country every week.

Use a keyword, phrase, or song to refocus and reset. We all have experienced what it feels like to be overwhelmed and discouraged. It's not easy, but try to view these feelings as opportunities to learn and reorganize. Scan your memory and think back to a time when you felt strong, empowered, peaceful, or safe. What was happening? Who was around? What was stimulating your senses? Identify what word or song resonates with these memories. This is now your "reset," your resilience on demand. Use it as a tool to reignite and reconnect with the energy it once took to rise up and persevere.

Find the positives, practice gratitude. You are not alone if you are currently feeling stressed, depressed, exhausted, or negative. At times, finding the positives can be a challenge. It may require you to "fake it till you make it." Challenge yourself to smile at least ten times a day. These smiles may not feel genuine, but they spark positivity and can release feel-good chemicals that help reduce stress and lift your mood. Give it a try! What do you have to lose?

Focus on what you can control and own. Begin to identify your response patterns and the level to which you internalize. Do you tend to take ownership of other people's feelings/actions, adjust to avoid conflict, or constantly compromise your needs for the needs of others? In order to change such tendencies, you must first learn to establish healthy boundaries. This step serves as a reminder to acknowledge your feelings and needs, which tend to be overshadowed by the intense desire to please and accommodate others.

Maintain a healthy lifestyle: Rest and restore. Prioritize the basics: Set yourself up for a good night's sleep, drink plenty of water throughout the day, be mindful of what you eat, and move your body. A healthy body and mind create a strong foundation and the resiliency it takes to move forward in life. Currently, people are working longer hours at home than they did in the office. To avoid burnout, you must schedule ample time to relax, disconnect from work, and be present with friends or family. Resilience can only be sustained when you set healthy boundaries and make the time to rejuvenate. Don't just go through the motions. Truly live life by being deliberate and present.

Embrace the idea that you will not always have all the answers, know how to react, or navigate an obstacle with grace. It is during these moments of uncertainty and challenge that extraordinary growth takes place, giving us the opportunity to observe how we bounce back and recover. Resilience is something you earn through practice and consistency. It requires a healthy mindset, time for reflection, and the ability to be present with your feelings.

Serial fixers often forget that people do not have the ability to access our every thought and emotion. The majority of individuals with debilitating anxiety are pros at hiding it and can appear cool and collected. People tend to be caught up in their own thoughts or are busy combating their anxieties. They simply do not have the space to hyperanalyze and excessively criticize you because they are overrun with their own internal tasks.

Practice giving yourself grace. Serial fixers are so quick to give others the benefit of the doubt but forget to share that same kindness with themselves. Anxious thoughts will not completely go away, but it can be managed and viewed as your mind's way to alert you. Validate the alert, but then practice managing anxiety rather than continuing to allow it to take full control of you.

Resilience

When I've asked past participants in my workshops to define resilience in their own words, here's what they've said:

"Always performing your best."
"Standing strong when life challenges you."
"Having the ability to move forward."
"Not breaking down or appearing weak."
"The strength to cope with various obstacles simultaneously."

Most people seem to associate resilience with consistently pushing forward, coping without emotionally breaking down, and succeeding time and time again. In my mind, however, all of these qualities ought to be more associated with stamina rather than resilience. Stamina is generally associated with sustaining physical exertion within a known block of time. For example, having the energy to finish a marathon or play all four quarters of the game with the same intensity and strength. Sports and physical competitions are scheduled and the duration or goal is common knowledge to those participating. There is training involved and time allotted for rest and recovery.

On the other hand, events or experiences that require resilience tend to occur without warning, lack a structured format, and follow unpredictable rules. Without time frames or clues to inform you about what may happen next, resiliency contrasts with stamina. A memorable example is the COVID-19 pandemic, which greatly impacted us socially, academically, politically, and economically. It was a long and intense journey, but one that also offered unique opportunities to pause, reflect, and rearrange priorities.

How do some people:

remain hopeful and creatively adapt?
push forward and live through life's hardships?
consistently access their resilience and avoid stagnation?

Genetic factors play a small role, but overall, resilience is something that is learned and acquired through action and perception. Life is not a sprint but rather a marathon through valleys, mountains, sunshine, and rain. Building resilience involves several steps that require time for reflection, acknowledgment, adjustment, and restoration. Those with high levels of self-awareness and self-connection often prove to be the most resilient.

We can persevere through difficult times and uncomfortable obstacles. The necessary tools are already something we possess and just need to be activated and nurtured.

Every time you challenge yourself and live with an open mind and open heart, you are increasing your repetitions and, in turn, building your confidence. As humans, we are meant to experience a full range of emotions. When we constantly suppress or avoid the difficult ones, it also becomes harder to fully access the extraordinary ones.

Positive Self-Talk

"I think, therefore I am."

You have most likely heard this famous quote by Descartes. But what happens when your feelings are so incredibly powerful that you can't quite access the "thinking" or "logical" part of your brain? What if you suddenly freeze when you long to communicate an idea or share an opinion? How can you execute and maintain presence when your mind becomes clouded with negativity, self-doubt, and apprehension?

Most of us believe we should strive for balance in our lives. However, the practice of rebalancing and resetting has been daunting for many, especially serial fixers. It requires consistently finding the space and energy to incorporate hope and positivity amid a steady stream of unknowns and difficult emotions.

When plagued by decision fatigue, it's healthy and proactive to respond by simplifying and resetting ourselves. Taking a step back allows us to mindfully sift through how our relationships, roles, and surroundings truly affect us. This time can be viewed as a time to cleanse and embrace the fact that we have control over the information, interactions, and pressures we allow into our lives. In doing so, we open the door to positive self-talk and affirmations that can guide us forward.

Helpful Mantras

- "I never have to do that day again."
- "I am doing my best, and that is enough."
- "It's okay to not have it all figured out."
- "I can learn from my mistakes."
- "I am worthy of kindness, including my own."

"I never have to do that day again" is a validating, comforting statement I have not only used myself but also shared with clients. It encourages embracing the here and now while adopting a mindset that balances disciplined progression with reasonable expectations. This approach affirms the efforts we invest daily. This is a form of self-compassion—an essential practice that is often not modeled or nurtured in childhood, especially for serial fixers. Learning and consistently applying this practice can be incredibly challenging in a society that not only pressures us to achieve but also glorifies stress and perfection. Acknowledging this struggle is crucial, as it reinforces the importance of being gentle with ourselves while we make changes. Practicing self-care involves deliberate activities that promote rejuvenation and relaxation. These practices reduce stress and reinforce the need to nurture ourselves and validate our daily efforts.

Self-compassion requires a mindset that combats anxiety, doubt, and unrealistic expectations. For serial fixers, being compassionate toward ourselves necessitates connection and self-love. It involves learning to forgive our mistakes and imperfections and viewing them as opportunities for growth. This worthwhile shift takes consistency and practice, ultimately helping clear emotional clutter and create space for deeper connections with ourselves and the world around us.

Regardless of how well we implement coping skills or take care of ourselves, we will encounter tough, complicated situations that impact us emotionally and compromise our stability or balance. Living under the belief that we can avoid pain, illness, and negative experiences through proactive measures only fuels unrealistic expectations and a misguided sense of control. Life is unpredictable, and our stories are often shaped by the choices of others, given our deep integration as social beings. This beautiful interconnectedness can, at times, become quite messy.

Living proactively rather than reactively requires, as you might guess, self-awareness and practice. By identifying your nonnegotiables and aligning your life with your values, you can help minimize overwhelming anxiety, sleep disturbances, and persistent negative self-talk. Practicing positive self-talk builds resilience and enhances your self-trust, helping you simplify your life and avoid engaging with the parts of yourself that focus too heavily on the future. Serial fixers typically struggle with this, but depending on your situation and age, what you need or desire in the form of recovery could change. This is where your check-ins come in handy. Collecting data and using it to implement changes and boundaries supports your relationship with yourself and others.

Self-compassion requires self-connection and forgiveness. Avoid using phrases like "I always" or "I never." Circumstances vary, and new conversations or events stimulate new feelings and thoughts. We must also embrace the fact that we do not show up or wake up feeling exactly the same way every day. Our energy levels are impacted by a number of factors, some in our control and some not.

Opportunity to Get a Rep In

For every negative thought or dismissal you give yourself, try to counter it with two positives. It might feel unnatural and inauthentic at first, but it gets easier with time. You are retraining your brain, and words do matter. If you're feeling daring or want to earn extra credit, consider looking in the mirror while you affirm these positive statements. This practice can deepen your self-connection and reinforce the affirmations you're cultivating.

We often forget that many external and internal sources influence how we feel, think, and therefore behave. The tone of our internal chatter truly matters. When we approach our day or a task with an open mind, we tend to avoid engaging with thought patterns that support negativity, doubt, and apprehension. Rather than categorizing life as "pass or fail" or "good or bad," view it as fluid and something that involves taking ownership when necessary. We tend to grow and learn the most when we experience uncertainty and discomfort. Continue to take positive risks and embrace the development and progression that will undoubtedly follow.

Practicing self-compassion requires us to adopt a framework that welcomes imperfection and embraces the importance of taking positive risks. It confirms that we should not be defined by the negative mishaps, decisions, or reactions that we've had and will continue to have from time to time. We possess the incredible capability to recover and learn, especially when we surrender control and refer to our past experiences in order to access the resilience we have already acquired. It is important to live proactively and make deliberate efforts to be healthy and balanced, but at the same time understand that these steps do not ultimately result in consistent success, safety, or good fortune. This journey of life is a dance, one that involves deliberation and perhaps a bit of luck.

One thing is for certain: We will continue to accompany ourselves throughout every step of our journey. Kindness and forgiveness should be prioritized. We are not supposed to have it all figured out at all times. Remember to validate and cherish all that you have navigated and achieved thus far.

What is "Real" Self-Care?

In recent years, the term *self-care* has become a cultural phenomenon—plastered across social media, touted in wellness blogs, and marketed as the ultimate remedy for stress and burnout. It's often depicted as indulgent spa days or expensive retreats, but despite its popularity, many people struggle to truly reap the benefits. Why? Because we've lost touch with what it really means to take care of ourselves. As a clinician, I've noticed that many people multitask even during their self-care routines, riddling these practices with distractions and diluting any real chance for recovery. Instead of recharging our batteries, we're scrolling through our phones, mentally running through to-do lists, or feeling guilty for taking time for ourselves. This disconnect leads to a misconstrued idea of what self-care should be, leaving us out of shape when it comes to being truly present.

The Misconception of Self-Care

Self-care is often portrayed as a luxury—something reserved for special occasions or when life becomes overwhelmingly stressful. It's easy to fall into the trap of believing that self-care needs to be a grand, expensive gesture. While certain luxurious activities or purchases can certainly be enjoyable, they can also set an unrealistic standard for what self-care is supposed to look like.

True self-care, however, doesn't require a large budget or a significant amount of time. It doesn't need to be extravagant or perfect. Real self-care is about simplicity and intention. It's about finding small, meaningful ways to check in with yourself regularly, even amid your daily responsibilities. Whether it's taking five minutes to breathe deeply, savoring a quiet moment with your morning coffee, or going for a short walk, self-care can—and should—fit seamlessly into your life.

The Importance of Presence

One of the most fundamental aspects of self-care is the ability to be fully present in the moment. In a world where distractions are constant, being present is often easier said than done. We live in an age where multitasking is celebrated, and productivity is prioritized above all else. But when it comes to self-care, this mindset can be counterproductive and can erase any of the true benefits.

Imagine taking a relaxing bath while simultaneously checking emails or scrolling through social media. While the intention might be to unwind, the reality is that your mind is still engaged in work or absorbing information—neither of which allows for true relaxation or recovery. This fragmented attention prevents the very benefits self-care is supposed to provide, leaving you feeling just as drained as before.

Presence requires mindfulness—fully engaging in the activity rather than focusing on what's next on your agenda. It's about slowing down and giving yourself permission to experience the moment fully. When you're present, even simple acts of self-care become powerful tools for rejuvenation. A short walk can become a moment of clarity, a few minutes of deep breathing can reset your nervous system, and a quiet cup of tea can turn into a peaceful ritual that nourishes your soul.

Consistency over Complexity

Another common misconception is that self-care needs to be time-consuming or elaborate. In reality, the most effective self-care practices are often the simplest ones—those that can be easily integrated into your daily routine. What matters most is consistency, not complexity. Taking advantage of the numerous transitions in your day and using them as times to reset or check in can do wonders not only for self-connection but also for clearing your inner clutter and embracing a new, mindful pace.

Self-care doesn't have to involve a lengthy meditation session or a perfectly curated routine. It's about finding small, manageable ways to care for yourself regularly. Consistency is key because it reinforces the habit of checking in with yourself and addressing your needs before they become overwhelming.

Consider the impact of just a few minutes each day dedicated to something that makes you feel good. It could be stretching in the morning, taking a few deep breaths before starting work, or enjoying a moment of silence during your lunch break. These small acts, when practiced consistently, can have a cumulative effect on your overall well-being. This is how we get into emotional shape!

By making self-care a regular part of your day, you build a foundation of resilience that helps you navigate life's challenges with greater ease. It's about prioritizing yourself in small, sustainable ways—ways that don't add stress but rather reduce it.

Internal Barriers to Self-Care

While it's easy to talk about the importance of self-care, actually implementing it can be a different story. Many of us struggle with internal barriers that limit our ability to fully engage in self-care, even when we recognize its value. These barriers often stem from deeply ingrained beliefs and habits—like self-criticism, guilt, or the pressure to always be productive.

For some, there's a persistent voice that says, "You don't deserve a break" or "There's too much to do to waste time on self-care." This InnerCritic can be powerful, convincing us that taking time for ourselves is selfish or indulgent. Others may feel guilty for stepping away from their responsibilities, even for a short time, as if doing so would somehow make them less competent or reliable.

These internal barriers are a significant reason why self-care can feel stressful rather than restorative. When you're battling against your own mind, even the simplest self-care practices can feel like a chore. The key to overcoming these barriers is to recognize them for what they are—protective mechanisms that have likely served you in some way in the past but are now preventing you from achieving balance and well-being.

Addressing these internal obstacles means challenging the notion that self-care is a luxury rather than a necessity. It's about giving yourself permission to care for your mental, emotional, and physical health without judgment. By doing so, you create space for genuine recovery and renewal, allowing you to return to your responsibilities with more energy and focus.

As you navigate the demands of daily life, keep in mind that self-care is not a reward to be earned but a necessity to be embraced. It doesn't have to be extravagant or time-consuming; it just has to be intentional. By focusing on presence and consistency, and by addressing the internal barriers that hold you back, you can unlock the true benefits of self-care—recharging your mind, body, and soul in ways that are both meaningful and, more importantly, sustainable.

The Serial Fixer's Guide to Structure (Not Perfection): The Four *S*'s

Regardless of whether you have your days completely mapped out in your quest as a serial fixer or are struggling to find your toothbrush in the morning amid your endless to-do list, the four *s*'s (sleep, sustenance, sweat, and silence) can serve as a guide to help you simplify the art of structuring your life in a healthy, constructive way. Rather than focusing on rigidity or overcommitting to others' needs, focus on understanding what you need to thrive, feel safe, and build confidence, allowing you to shift from fixing everyone else's problems to nurturing your own well-being.

Sleep

Setting yourself up for a good night's sleep involves establishing boundaries and being mindful of your behaviors and choices as you wind down for the evening. Just like parents create sacred sleep routines for their children, adults also need to prioritize their sleep routines and establish mindful boundaries.

During the evening hours, it's important to be aware of mental distractions like excessive screen time or food and drinks that may provide temporary comfort or reward. These behaviors can interfere with the quality of your sleep and hinder your ability to unwind effectively. Creating a sleep routine and setting boundaries around it can significantly contribute to a restful night's sleep and a more manageable day ahead. Consider implementing activities that promote relaxation and signal to your brain that it's time to wind down. This may include reading a book, practicing a calming mindfulness or meditation exercise, taking a warm bath, or engaging in a relaxing hobby. The activity might make no sense to anyone else. You'll know it's the right activity, however, if it effectively creates the second bookend to your day.

One boundary to discuss further is limiting your screen time, particularly in the evening. The blue light emitted by electronic devices has been known to disrupt your sleep-wake cycle and make it harder for you to fall asleep. Aim to establish a designated time to disconnect from screens, allowing your brain to unwind and prepare for sleep. Instead, engage your curiosity to find other activities which promote relaxation and a soothing atmosphere before bed.

Being mindful of what you consume before bed is also important. Avoid heavy meals, caffeine, and stimulants close to bedtime, as they will interfere with your ability to fall and stay asleep. Choose lighter, easily digestible foods and consider calming herbal teas instead of caffeinated beverages. You've likely heard these tips before, but I hope you are learning new reasons to put them in place. Start by paying attention to your habits and what quality of sleep they lead to. You will likely find that changing one behavior can have an outside impact on your rest. You may also learn that these evening habits were only providing you with temporary relief, only to sabotage you later. Gaining an understanding of how you categorize certain vices and distractions is crucial.

What do I feel?
What will this do for me?
What am I trying to distract myself from?

What am I attempting to satisfy or validate?
What are my options at this moment?
Did I check in with myself today?
Did I not have a chance to process or debrief?

Being mindful of your evening behaviors, you can create an environment that supports a restful night's sleep. Each person's sleep routine varies, so find what works best for you and stick to it. Prioritize your sleep, and you'll likely notice the positive impact it has on your overall well-being and daily functioning. Recognizing and addressing the emotional clutter and baggage we carry is the precursor for supporting restful sleep.

Engaging in regular check-ins with yourself throughout the day allows you to assess your emotional state, identify any stressors or concerns, and take proactive steps to address them. Give yourself permission to let go of any built-up tension or emotions, similar to letting the air out of a balloon. Suppressing or disregarding these feelings leads to an accumulation of stress and emotional burden, which often manifests when you're quiet or trying to sleep.

For many, nighttime is when the brain activates to surface unresolved stressors or emotions. Maybe it's replaying something you said earlier that you now realize was awkward or dumb. Perhaps it's the argument you lost or the question you answered wrong in a meeting. Or maybe it's that nagging feeling of forgetting to respond to someone's email, leaving you worried about how it might have been perceived. This disruption hinders sleep and impacts overall well-being. Unless we create dedicated pockets of time during our day to validate and address our feelings or problems, the brain will take it upon itself to clear the clutter, at inopportune times. Unresolved emotions and stressors frequently surface when the brain isn't distracted by daytime activities. During sleep, especially in REM sleep, the brain processes emotions and consolidates memories, which can cause emotional and stressful thoughts to emerge late at night if they haven't been addressed earlier.

Finding healthy outlets for emotional release, such as journaling, talking to a trusted friend or therapist, engaging in creative pursuits, or practicing mindfulness techniques are what create these pockets of self-reflection and validation. I had a client years ago who benefited from the suggestion to keep a notebook on her nightstand. When she found herself lying awake at two a.m., consumed by work-related worries, she would lean over, jot down the racing concerns (validating them), and then set a boundary with herself by cycling through these questions:

What can I control?
What are my options?
What can I let go of?
What is my role?

This process helped her put things into perspective and access some logic, even though doing so in the middle of the night is challenging, as the logical parts of our brain are essentially shut down, resetting for the next day. This approach takes practice. If you want to try this yourself, don't use your phone, as that would only stimulate you further and lead to additional distractions.

I've shared this suggestion with many of the athletes who see me for therapy. Athletes often struggle to soothe their Inner-Critic and transition away from mistakes they made in practice or missed opportunities in a game. I encourage them to validate and acknowledge the feelings but also set internal boundaries and maintain presence. Many athletes find it helpful to keep a notebook in their bag or locker, and after practice or a game, they write down how they're feeling, what they can control, what they've learned, and conclude by reciting their personal motto. For example, "One practice or one game doesn't define me" or "I can recover, and I trust myself." Some athletes like to keep a record of these reflections, using the act of closing the notebook and walking out of the gym, off the field, or out of the locker room as a cue to move on—symbolizing closure. Others prefer ripping up the page, finding symbolism in throwing it away and transitioning with renewed focus.

These exercises not only help you get your reps in but also build self-trust and soothe the parts of yourself that tend to seek attention. Find what works best for you and build toward consistently integrating these practices into your routine. By actively addressing and validating your emotions and concerns when you're functioning at your best, you reduce the chances of them resurfacing when you're trying to sleep.

Sustenance

Nourishing your body involves understanding your overall relationship with food and how it influences how you feel about your body. There are countless frameworks that attempt to help you maintain a weight that is healthy for you and feel as energetic and connected as you can. Researching these can be overwhelming. Implementing some sort of diet structure can be helpful, but not if it encourages rigidity and moves you in a direction that does not encourage you to listen to your body and value it as you would a teammate. Your body is on your team. If you listen closely, it will guide you as it wants nothing more than for you to be the best version of yourself. It's no secret that drinking enough water is one of the easiest and strongest contributors to overall well-being, yet consistently integrating it into your day can be a struggle. I encourage my clients to view water as their foundation to cleanse, fuel, and activate.

Food is another common quick fix or distraction. When certain feelings become too intense, and we don't have the appropriate space to release them, the mind becomes a scavenger.

It cycles through available options that could help soothe or divert difficult feelings. Sometimes we use food or beverages as rewards or symbols of enjoyment. This is fine for most in moderation, especially if you make an effort to be present while eating for its enjoyment. Sugar and alcohol for example are two primary sources that most of us associate with a certain time of day or type of event.

We might justify this behavior with thoughts like

"I need this to transition into another part of my day."
"It helps me feel relaxed."
"I worked hard and deserve it."
"This symbolizes relief or a good time, and I shouldn't have to go without it."

Some foods and drinks are so tied to our culture and family traditions that giving them up can feel like losing part of ourselves. Taking time to reflect on your habits and choices can help you stay healthy while staying true to who you are.

Sweat

It's important to note that incorporating movement and exercise into our lives doesn't necessarily mean grueling workouts or strict training regimens. The key is finding consistent activities that you enjoy and that suit your individual preferences and capabilities.

While movement and exercise take various forms, you must strike a balance between listening to your body's needs and pushing yourself within safe limits. It's easy to fall into the trap of using exercise as a means to impress or validate our self-worth, but this approach quickly becomes detrimental and hinders us from fully experiencing the benefits of movement. Finding sources of structure and guidance, such as workout programs or fitness classes, help create frameworks for our exercise routines. They provide a sense of direction and ensure that we engage in a well-rounded and balanced routine.

However, it's important to be mindful not to become overly rigid or robotic in our approach. Overexerting yourself or chasing unrealistic goals can lead to injury, burnout, and a strained relationship with exercise. It's important to listen to your body, adjust your workouts as needed, and honor rest days for proper recovery. Engaging in movement should be primarily driven by self-care and enjoyment, rather than seeking validation or trying to impress others. By shifting your focus to how exercise makes you feel rather than how it makes you look, you can cultivate a healthier and more sustainable relationship with physical activity.

Listening to your body, finding joy in movement, and embracing a balanced approach to exercise allows you to reap the full benefits of staying active. It helps you build strength, improve cardiovascular fitness, enhance flexibility, and boost your mental and emotional well-being. It also reduces the risk of injury and prevents burnout, ensuring that we can continue to engage in physical activity for the long term. Serial fixers must find the sweet spot between challenging themselves and respecting their body's limits.

During my graduate studies, I experienced a shift familiar to many serial fixers. With my collegiate basketball days behind me, I struggled with the transition. Though I kept up my workouts, which had always given me confidence and a sense of accomplishment, I felt an underlying stress. One day, I called my mom, overwhelmed by deadlines and pressure, and ending the call with a determined plan to go for a run. However, my plan was rigid. The run had to be a specific distance, at a certain speed, and I expected to feel immediate relief afterward. I was placing intense pressure on this run, almost using it as a test to validate my worth as an athlete and a capable person.

My mom, also a psychotherapist, listened patiently and then challenged my rigid approach. She asked, "What if you just went for a run and listened to your body as you went? No rules, no plan, just run." At first, I resisted, but as I considered her words, I realized that I had fallen out of practice when it came to simply existing. My past experiences instilled a sense of competition and high stakes which I continued to apply to everything. I needed to give myself grace, remain present, and balance that with some structure. Taking her advice was challenging at first. My InnerCritic was not pleased, but I learned that finding harmony between listening to my body and pursuing my goals was indeed possible. This experience helped to soothe my InnerCritic, reduce pressure, and build self-trust.

Many serial fixers, especially those who have been part of a team, experience grief when the structure of their previous pursuits shifts or ends. This transition can significantly impact their sense of identity, comfort, and overall well-being. For many, their primary source of identity and purpose becomes intricately tied to their accomplishments, providing a sense of belonging and routine. When that structure changes—whether due to career shifts, personal setbacks, or other circumstances—they may find themselves navigating a profound sense of loss. The absence of the familiar routines and dynamics that once motivated and supported them can lead to feelings of emptiness.

The grieving process is often overlooked but must be recognized and navigated thoughtfully by serial fixers. Neglecting these emotional transitions can undermine confidence, self-esteem, and a sense of purpose. During this period, it becomes important to cultivate sources of validation and self-worth beyond past roles. Exploring new facets of identity—whether through hobbies, varied physical activities, or avenues of personal and professional growth—can offer renewed fulfillment and a deeper sense of purpose.

Recognizing and addressing the psychological and emotional aspects of these transitions enables them to navigate changes with greater resilience and maintain a positive sense of self. The journey to redefine one's identity beyond previous pursuits is unique and deeply personal, and providing the necessary support can significantly enhance overall well-being and success in this next chapter.

Silence

Setting aside at least a few minutes every day without distractions can significantly improve your mental health and your ability to be present in life. Whether you meditate, unplug from your devices, or take a quiet walk, time alone fosters increased self-awareness. Sensory silence offers a valuable opportunity to reflect and reconnect with yourself—a practice that requires patience and dedication.

In the midst of a busy sensory world, moments of silence and stillness become important ingredients to overall well-being. Dedicate time each day for reflection, meditation, or mindfulness practices. Disconnect from external stimuli and embrace the present moment. Engaging in silence promotes mental clarity, reduces stress, and cultivates inner peace. Find practices that resonate with you and integrate them into your daily routine.

This doesn't require adding something new. Think about all the transitions you experience throughout the day, whether physical or mental. View these transitions as opportunities to check in with yourself and your surroundings. Ask yourself:

How am I feeling?
How does my body feel?
Where are the themes of my thoughts?
How am I responding to my environment or situation?

There is no judgment here. Refrain from judgment or negative self-talk even when your answers are not ideal or uncomfortable. The goal is to gather data, wipe your slate clean. Initially, you might not experience relief, connection, or clarity at all, or you might feel it for only a few seconds. Keep at it! This practice takes reps, so be patient. You are building connections with yourself and identifying behavior and thought patterns with each effort.

If you spend a lot of time in the car, instead of using the pauses at red lights to check messages or social updates, treat them as opportunities for mindfulness. Scan with your five senses, embrace your childlike curiosity, and just observe. Even if you've been at the same intersection countless times, there's always something new to notice. As you embrace this practice, tap into your senses. Pay attention to how you feel, what you see, and what you hear. Use this moment to take a few deep breaths and ground yourself in the present, affirming that you are here, now. This easy-to-use mindfulness exercise can be done throughout the day, but associating it with a specific routine or situation helps create the habit. This strong connection is something your brain will understand and can capitalize on. Over time, you'll reap the benefits.

Finally, time in silence can literally retrain our brains. Imagine your mind as a network of tunnels, some harboring anxiety and self-doubt, that is well-worn due to heavy traffic. In contrast, those tunnels associated with optimism and confidence often need nurturing since they may be underused. Regularly engaging in mindfulness practices can help pave new pathways, promoting a healthier and more balanced mental landscape.

When apprehension arises, view it as an opportunity to choose which tunnel you'll venture down. Take a breath and acknowledge that this is the moment the battle begins. Rewiring your thinking patterns and fighting negative self-talk requires a tremendous amount of strength—but each second you push back, you're gaining a rep. You're strengthening a tunnel that encourages positive self-talk and, with time, traveling down this path will require less effort. It will eventually become more automatic.

By implementing the four *s*'s of structure—sleep, sustenance, sweat, and silence—serial fixers can begin to establish a framework supporting their well-being on multiple levels. These pillars provide a solid foundation for physical vitality, mental clarity, emotional balance, and overall resilience. Integrate these practices as essential components of your lifestyle, and you will experience their transformative power to enhance your well-being.

Indeed, the pursuit of well-being is not about striving for perfection but rather about finding rhythms and routines that bring out the best parts of yourself. It is through these intentional practices that you can create self-awareness and a sense of fulfillment. When you focus on nurturing your authentic self, you shift your emphasis from seeking external validation to fostering internal validation.

Rhythms and routines provide stability and a sense of grounding in your life. They create a framework so you can prioritize activities and practices that align with your values and aspirations. This intentional approach allows you to focus on personal growth and self-improvement, nurturing the qualities and strengths that make you unique.

Get your reps in whether it's in the gym or by drinking water, but remind yourself that this becomes more ingrained and beneficial when you partner it with validation. Acknowledge your efforts and abilities to maintain consistency. This enhances feelings associated with self-worth and is yet another way to contribute to your resilience bank. By nurturing your authentic self and finding rhythms and routines that resonate, you cultivate a stronger sense of self-confidence and self-acceptance. You continue to learn how to trust your judgment and make choices that align with your true desires and aspirations. It's important to note that finding rhythms and routines that encourage the best parts of yourself to shine is a personal journey. Each person's path will be unique, and it requires self-exploration and self-reflection to discover what works best for you. It may involve trial and error but approach this process with patience, compassion, and a willingness to adapt and adjust as needed.

Chapter 7

Ditching False Ownership and Codependency

False ownership refers to the tendency to take on the burdens, challenges, or problems of others that are not your own. This behavior often stems from weak boundaries and a compulsion to fix or solve for others, traits commonly found in serial fixers. False ownership can significantly affect your well-being and hinder your ability to set and maintain healthy boundaries. Those who struggle with false ownership may find themselves overidentifying with others, leading to imbalanced relationships where support is not reciprocated. This dynamic can create a safe zone, or a false sense of security, that prevents vulnerability and genuine connection.

False Ownership

Over the years, I've facilitated numerous groups aimed at increasing self-awareness and helping individuals reconnect with their purpose. Many participants want to actively engage in their lives learning to distinguish what is truly theirs to own and what they need to reframe or release. These groups have included athletes, teachers, mentors, C-suite leaders, and a virtual collective I co-facilitate for professional women. This group offers a space for women to understand and work with their InnerCritic while breaking the recurring cycle of burnout. These participants balance a variety of personal and professional roles, including motherhood, and have achieved success across multiple areas. Yet despite their perseverance and motivation, many feel disconnected from a deeper sense of fulfillment.

They strive for success as mothers but often struggle to create space and establish boundaries that grant their children the independence needed for growth. As a result, they find themselves constantly managing tasks while their children learn to depend on their proactive efforts. This sometimes leaves little room for their children to develop skills like problem-solving, emotional regulation, or handling mistakes independently. While these highly capable parents may not entirely compromise their kids' resilience, the opportunities for such growth become limited. As their children become young adults, some struggle to function without the structured parental support they once had. Meanwhile, these women face a new dilemma: strategically navigating professional transitions or hurdles in intimate relationships while grappling with the question, Why do I feel the urge to parent more than ever? Despite their children having grown and moved out on their own, these women are left wondering, "Why am I struggling with loneliness, an inability to set boundaries, or to thrive independently?"

These struggles become the basis for evaluating their success as parents. This creates a sense of urgency to fix and alleviate their child's pain, not only for their child's sake but also to soothe their own ego. They make frequent check-in calls to their kids and offer unsolicited advice and criticism. This pattern triggers anxiety and a sense of failure for both parties involved. These women, like most parents, just want a positive relationship with their kids, but they aren't sure how to build it.

In these groups, we spend several sessions exploring how high levels of empathy and a strong drive to succeed can lead to false ownership. This is when egos take charge, and individuals begin to use others' issues as a measure of their own effectiveness. False ownership involves taking on someone else's experience, choices, or problems without understanding your role or whether you even have one. While it comes from a place of care and protective intentions, it can have the opposite effect. False ownership often arises from a deep emotional investment in the other person's well-being and success, but this investment can cloud judgment. Parts of you shaped by past experiences, such as childhood, directly influence your values, fears, and hopes as an adult. When these emotions become too intense, they can distort your perception and make it difficult for the other person to fully engage in their own process or learn from their experiences. This projection of your own issues can impede their growth, as you inadvertently take over the responsibility they need to claim for themselves.

Rather than approaching conversations with their children with curiosity, these women can fall victim to the urge to direct and control. Their excessive investment impacts their relationships and other areas of their lives. Much of their energy is dedicated to fixing and solving, in order to relieve themselves from the wrath of their InnerCritic.

Someone who constantly takes false ownership typically faces symptoms of anxiety. It's a heavy load to process someone else's emotions and issues while scanning for how you may have contributed to their experience. But it doesn't have to be this way. You will soon learn to implement the "Support, Don't Solve" framework to help identify your tendencies and navigate conversations with your empathy intact but without the burden of taking on someone else's emotions.

I've had to work hard to avoid taking on false responsibility, even from a young age. Like most children, I looked forward to my birthday—a special day marked by celebration. I was fortunate to have a party or some form of celebration each year, and the anticipation always filled me with excitement. But once my friends began to arrive, that excitement quickly turned into anxious thoughts.

I felt an overwhelming pressure to make sure everyone was having a good time. Even as a seven-year-old, I carried an unrealistic expectation to control and cater to everyone's needs, which often kept me from enjoying my own celebration. I got wrapped up in false narratives and endless comparisons. I exhausted myself by trying to monitor everyone's expressions and energy, believing I had to keep everyone happy. This pattern didn't end with my seventh birthday. It followed me into caretaking relationships and a career where I sought to soothe or feel needed, often at the expense of my own well-being.

While I was able to enjoy being a kid, I lacked the understanding to identify my role and release the pressure to accommodate everyone. I tried as best as I could to avoid gossip and social competition. Those things were too intense and drove my need to fix and solve, which usually did not end well. I couldn't yet respect that I had no knowledge of how the last twenty-four hours of my friends' lives had played out. Perhaps they didn't sleep well or they got into an argument with a sibling that changed their mood and energy level. Maybe they became nervous when they found out we were going skating or that they might not know everyone at my party. All of these factors and emotions were not mine and did not need to be fixed by me unless someone specifically asked me to step in. I was making my friend's well-being my responsibility and taking false ownership which left little room for mine.

It is possible to lead with empathy while maintaining presence and defusing the anxiety that tends to be ignited with the need to control or feel externally validated. This understanding has helped me navigate relationships and work with a healthier balance, allowing me to be empathetic without falling into the trap of false ownership.

What People Say About You Is None of Your Business

I had just entered my teen years and was navigating middle school—a time when most of us start to sharpen our social assessment skills. We become more aware of what others might be thinking, our egos swell, and our thoughts can become laced with a touch of paranoia. Am I liked? Am I original enough but still able to fit in? Am I good enough? Are people analyzing me? These questions drifted through my mind constantly throughout the week.

One day, as I maneuvered through the chaotic swarm of seventh graders to find my locker, I noticed a group of girls glancing in my direction. As I turned the dial and opened my locker, I casually looked up again to confirm it: They were indeed looking at me and whispering to each other. My mind immediately latched onto a negative train of thought, and I could feel my body heat up. Is it my outfit? Did I say something weird in fourth period? Am I liked? Am I good enough? These questions plagued me for the rest of the day.

After basketball practice, my mom and grandma picked me up, and I collapsed into the car. I was not only physically exhausted from the endless sprints we'd run but also emotionally drained. I had spent the entire day replaying the scene in the hallway, fueling my inner turmoil. Despite listening to lessons and laughing with friends at lunch, I multitasked through it all, my mind frantically trying to piece together what might have been said or thought about me.

My grandma asked me how my day was and seemed to pick up on my mood and dilemma when I provided an abrupt and minimal response. She pressed, and I told them what happened in the hallway. My grandma listened, paused, and said, "Hmm. It sounds like you've given this a lot of thought. Even if those girls said something about you, we can't be sure, but it is actually none of your business."

What? None of my business? It's about me! I was potentially the main attraction, the subject of their enjoyment and petty bonding experience. How does that not concern me? Silently, I gave my grandma the benefit of the doubt, telling myself it was a nice effort, but she went to middle school decades ago—things had obviously changed. Little did I know that this small piece of wisdom, her unexpected response, would come back to me many times as I navigated my adult life.

I had allowed myself to make a number of ignorant assumptions which led to anxious thoughts and a state of slight paranoia. My InnerPleaser was sounding the alarm and my InnerCritic was sifting through every mistake and weird statement I made since birth. Rather than walk away, I asked my grandma for clarification in a typical teenage form: "Huh?"

She replied, "What people say about you is none of your business. If you are not in the conversation, it doesn't pertain to you. It might be about you, but it is not your business." I let this sink in, and over time, I was able to connect the dots and understand how the anxiety spiral I experienced that day could have been avoided. I was taking false ownership and creating false narratives that didn't impact anyone except me. She went on to explain that I needed to trust that if someone wanted to share something with me, they would approach me. I could allow hypotheticals and the *potential* words of others to dictate my mood, or I could surrender to not being in control of what others think. The concept takes time, but it is something I have actively honed ever since that day.

Codependency

Adopting and applying the "Support, Don't Solve" approach has been invaluable for protecting my boundaries in both my professional life and personal relationships, particularly in my marriage.

Over the seventeen years of our relationship, my husband and I faced a steep learning curve. Before meeting my husband, I saw myself as an effective communicator—laid-back, highly empathetic, and with established boundaries. These traits gave me confidence in navigating relationships, yet I often struggled with a tendency to overplease and caretake, sacrificing my own needs and desires in pursuit of connection, love, and validation.

I could anticipate his triggers and, for a while, set my insecurities aside. However, my strategy had its limits. My hidden emotions would eventually surface, leading to internal battles that remained on my mind and began to challenge the core pillars of the life we had already built together. The narratives I created during these times overwhelmed me. I would often unload this disarray of thoughts on him without warning, leaving him feeling confused and overwhelmed, which ultimately led to him shutting down. The internal conflict I faced grew even more intense as I tried to balance caring for my husband while also advocating for myself.

My InnerCritic and InnerRescuer were at war. My InnerCritic wanted me to advocate for myself and not take any nonsense. My InnerRescuer joined forces with my InnerPleaser to defuse the guilt and soothe the repeated motto that circulated through my thoughts: Do no harm. This scene would unravel and create a distance that usually lasted for several days. We wouldn't yell or argue; there was just silence. I felt dismissed and ignored as we went about our routines without acknowledging or giving the other the privilege of joining in. This was new to me, and it ate at me in ways that seemed unbearable.

I needed to make sure that he was okay and that my emotions and venting didn't hurt him, or worse, make him fall out of love with me. The urgency and anxiety led me to circle back way too much. I wanted him to share. I wanted to be the listener and needed him to be okay so that I could be too. I didn't fully understand this dynamic, which led to internalizing and taking false ownership of, well, everything. "Are you okay?" "How are you feeling?" "I'm sorry for dumping all of that on you."

I would apologize and wish that I could take all of what I shared back, even though it needed to come out. The look on his face as he would shut down and disengage haunted me. The responses or lack of responses I would receive would feed my InnerCritic. Why can't I get a grasp on this? Am I too needy? I must be expecting too much. I am being ungrateful. The silence that once fueled anxiety began to irritate me. My InnerRescuer occupied more space, and I could feel the athlete inside me flex and take a stand: "Oh, we're playing this game, huh? Well, I just need to work with what I have and be proactive in filling the gaps that are now part of my world."

In those moments, what would soothe me—yet perpetuate the unhealthy pattern—were words of validation. Words that calmed my ego and reframed the essence of our relationship as hopeful and positive. This reassurance would momentarily stop my tendency to compare and feel as though I had to "do without" or "make do" due to the gaps in our communication. Logically, I knew that every marriage has its challenges and that most of the challenges I experienced were scenarios that I had helped many of my clients navigate, too. I entered my marriage with the realistic expectation that he would not be the solution to everything and fulfill my every need. I would be responsible for creating goals, fueling other relationships, and taking care of myself. I needed to continue to nurture my friendships and find hobbies that didn't need to involve him. Logically, this all made sense, yet it was more difficult to convince my emotional side.

These occasional awkward silences disrupted the usual beat of our household. Juggling my roles as a clinician, mom, coach, and friend left me exhausted, and even sleep—a typical reset—was affected until we would connect and move forward. This pattern continued until we gradually learned to set boundaries and manage expectations, marked by moments that shared familiar challenges but also reflected our growing improvement. I began to trust his word when he said he was "fine" or "okay," instead of pressing for more or letting my ego interpret his nonverbal reactions as a reflection of me. While I still checked in and kept communication open, I had to accept that sometimes the ball was in his court.

Initially, this approach felt cold, challenging the notion that his happiness reflected my success. However, I came to understand that creating space for connection wasn't just about when he wanted it—it required mutual understanding and respect for both our needs. This shift helped break the pattern of overworking for emotional reassurance. Despite occasional ups and downs, my marriage has been an incredible teacher. Our weekly coffee dates serve as a constant, symbolizing two separate yet deeply connected journeys.

We're two cars on the same highway, aware that the journey may have pit stops or detours. Reconnecting is essential, but it doesn't require being in the same car with the same route. Our union is unique and our responsibility. We aim to nurture each other and our children while avoiding the expectation of anticipating every need. Instead, we focus on tending to our individual "vehicles," cultivating a relationship rooted in love, mutual respect, and individual growth.

I've learned to implement this with my children too. I have always aimed (and will always aim) to create space for them when they are experiencing a mood dip or a challenge. When I take the time to check in with myself and understand where my urge to fix or solve comes from, I can better respect my children's ability to self-soothe and overcome challenges on their own. Just like me, my kids need to get their reps in. My role is to guide and provide structure, to show love and support—not to overaccommodate or shield them from the full range of emotions that are a natural part of being human.

Ask yourself what your true motivator is when you repeatedly ask someone if they are okay. Perhaps you've already received a response like, "I'm okay" or "I need some space," but their mood or nonverbal communication does not align. You are desperately working to assuage their pain even though you may have had a hand in triggering it. These situations are difficult for empaths to believe and can summon their InnerPleaser. The need to be needed and to regain balance is intense and drives efforts that unfortunately usually make the situation worse for the person who needs space to internally process. You poke and prod, driven by the guilt of feeling solely responsible for your loved one's emotions. In those moments, it's hard to access logic and recognize that the cues or boundaries set by them may have nothing to do with you. They may have been raised in a family that didn't share their feelings or externally process. They may have been ridiculed or felt unsafe. They may fear that their anger will overarch all of their feelings and they need space to get a handle on what they're experiencing.

Learning to trust that someone is telling you the truth when they say they're okay takes reps. Only they can take ownership of whether their communication with you is in alignment with how they truly feel. You can circle back, but be mindful of your timing and be real with your motivation. Learning to self-soothe in these moments of disconnect can be incredibly challenging. It's helpful to **fact-check** and call yourself out on any catastrophic or all-or-nothing thought patterns. When you pause and maintain presence during these moments, you can take ownership of what is

> **fact-check**—A technique to balance emotional responses by identifying objective facts, helping to add logic to anxious or overwhelming thoughts.

truly yours and attempt to let go of the need to control and be soothed. Identifying themes is helpful and one of the premises of my therapeutic work but this practice is most effective when a healthy balance of logic and emotion has been achieved. If urgency, guilt, shame, and anxiety are driving your thoughts, it is important to pause and revisit introspection later.

Fact-check. Remember to:
Identify your motivator.
Take ownership of your role.
Honor others' boundaries.
Share what setup or structure may work better in the future to defuse triggers on both ends.

The mind quickly tries to fill the gaps, but the ego tends to make its way into this filter, reframing everything to be about you. All-or-nothing thinking is highly likely when we are operating with a sense of urgency and angst. Your focus begins to stray, and rather than staying present with the current situation and the facts at hand, you skip ahead and perhaps over analyze the entire relationship, challenge how much you are loved, and wonder if you are even worthy enough to be in this partnership. Sometimes you linger here, and sometimes your anger filters through the ego and switches to a protective mode, causing you to think this person is not worthy of you or to wonder how they could be so sensitive and not know how to communicate effectively. These thoughts are not only exhausting but they fuel your need to be needed and receive confirmation that you are still liked, loved, and worthy. When we fill in the gaps with our own negative, anxiety-driven lens, it becomes even harder to manage these emotions.

A hallmark of a serial fixer is quickly taking ownership or trying to remove the burden of a task that could cause discomfort. This tendency comes from a place of love and empathy but can also be an attempt to relieve others' own discomfort or make life a bit easier. Serial fixers step in to solve the problems of others close to them, but this can stifle growth and create enmeshed dependent relationships. A space creator, on the other hand, must tap into patience and discern whether they have the resources to help without taking over. Working through the steps *alongside* others gives them the opportunity to build confidence and independence. When we peel back the layers, we see that the ego plays a significant role in these dynamics. Using others' emotions and struggles to validate ourselves, confirm that we're needed, or distract from our own issues makes it difficult to cultivate authentic connection and peace.

Adulting and Friendships: The Struggle Is Real

Navigating the landscape of adult friendships can be complex and influenced by many factors. The fast pace of modern life, filled with demanding jobs, family responsibilities, and numerous commitments, often leaves little space for meaningful social interactions. In the past, the structure of traditional educational systems created plenty of opportunities to connect with peers who shared similar roles and schedules.

In adulthood, our roles, schedules, and responsibilities vary widely, leaving us with the task of actively structuring our social lives and taking risks to seek connections. For those dealing with social anxiety or shyness, the fear of judgment and rejection becomes a significant barrier, making it especially challenging to initiate conversations or participate in social activities.

For these reasons and more, we tend to turn to social media or interactions through our devices, which creates the illusion that we are connected, even though we're not. The allure of online interactions draws us away from face-to-face relationships, which require more effort. As a result, many of us grapple with feelings of inadequacy, doubting our ability to form and maintain meaningful friendships and becoming hesitant to reach out. However, relying on digital connections can ultimately lead to loneliness and a false sense of comfort, diminishing our motivation to explore, take risks, and satisfy the natural urge to expand our social circles and experiences.

Constant change, whether relocating for a job or undergoing significant personal events, can disrupt established social circles, leaving individuals with the challenge of creating new connections as they heal and adjust. The momentum and trust required to build healthy relationships can be continually interrupted, leading to feelings of resentment and the belief that you don't need others and can handle everything on your own. We are wired for connection, and this mindset can leave us with false narratives and perpetuate negativity and disconnect with events, experiences, and purpose.

What about personality traits, codependent tendencies, and unresolved internal issues? Many adults find themselves in relationships that replicate familiar patterns of dependency because they avoid processing the aftermath of a stressful relationship. Sometimes, we take the "distraction" route, diving into the excitement of new relationships to mask our confusion or pain. However, more often than not, these new relationships end up reflecting the same patterns and dynamics.

What are some of the key components that can interfere with cultivating healthy relationships?

Low self-esteem. Those with low self-esteem may accept unequal treatment in friendships because they feel they don't deserve better or fear losing the friendship if they assert themselves.

Lack of boundaries. A person who struggles to set and enforce boundaries may find themselves in imbalanced friendships. Without clear boundaries, others may take advantage or not recognize the limits of acceptable behavior.

Mismatched expectations. Differences in expectations about the nature of the friendship can lead to imbalances. If one person expects more commitment or investment than the other, it can result in feelings of being taken for granted.

Narcissistic or manipulative behavior. Individuals with narcissistic tendencies may exploit others for their own gain. They may seek out friendships where they can dominate or use the other person for their needs without reciprocating.

Fear of confrontation. Some individuals avoid confrontation at all costs, even if it means tolerating unfair treatment. This fear can lead to a pattern of being taken advantage of without addressing the issue.

Social isolation or desperation for friendship. Someone who feels socially isolated or desperately seeks companionship may be more willing to tolerate imbalanced friendships out of fear of being alone.

Unhealthy relationship patterns. Individuals who have experienced imbalanced relationships in the past, such as in their family or romantic relationships, may inadvertently replicate these patterns in future relationships.

Relationships are complex, particularly those requiring deeper levels of connection and intimacy. Building and nurturing relationships, like anything else, takes reps and the work involved in understanding your tendencies. Creating your own opportunities to meet people may seem intimidating, but pulling from your resilience bank and taking a few risks socially could go a long way. Perhaps take a look at what is happening in your community and reconnect. Explore local events or reconnect with the parts of yourself you've kept hidden, like your playful or adventurous side.

What interests you? What are you drawn to? What new experience could you try? Fight back against keeping your world too steady, safe, and predictable. You are capable of more and have much more to offer and receive. Stand tall, walk tall, and take up space.

As we navigate the intricate dynamics of relationships, whether professional or personal, the interplay of false ownership, codependency, and the urge to fix can undermine our ability to cultivate healthy connections. Serial fixers tend to take on the emotional burdens of others. This tendency stems from a deep-seated desire for validation, leading them to confuse empathy with an obligation to solve problems for others. This inclination perpetuates unhealthy dynamics and feeds their fears of inadequacy and rejection, stifling genuine connection. By recognizing the importance of honoring personal boundaries and allowing others the space to process their feelings we can break the cycle of dependency that fuels anxiety and guilt. Embracing our role in relationships means understanding what we can control while respecting what lies beyond our influence.

Chapter 8

Maintaining Presence and Creating Space

Space is a word that mental health professionals often use when discussing topics such as psychological safety and self-rejuvenation. Creating the space necessary to reflect, reset, or simply rest is essential to our well-being and improves the connection with not only ourselves but others as well.

Creating Space for Yourself

Becoming a space creator involves generating space for others, but it must also involve creating space for yourself. This is the area that most are likely to under appreciate in favor of serving others' needs over our own. We tend to make decisions through the filter of our powerful InnerPleaser to accommodate others and feel needed. We often use others' needs or obstacles to give structure to our own lives, reinforcing our sense of connection through solving their problems. While this can be a beautiful and meaningful way to connect, it can lead to burnout and compassion fatigue if not carefully monitored and balanced.

Your individual needs are overpowered by your intense need to be needed. When opportunities to fill the needs of others are not available, you might create them in a subconscious effort to avoid the energy it takes to focus on your own healing or growth. The pull to please leads you further and further away from connecting with yourself. Your basic needs might be covered and checked off on a daily basis, but you don't take the time to check in and validate your own emotions or thought processes, which only fuels disconnect and anxiety. A structure built on anticipating others' potential judgements, needs, or thoughts becomes the main source of your decision-making. It becomes more and more challenging to maintain presence and experience a sense of calm. Your mind tends to be overloaded, and you struggle to just be in the here and now. The busy mind craves high levels of stimulation, but this stimulation overshadows opportunities to connect with yourself and what you are currently experiencing.

Many of the clients I have worked with in the past are incredible space creators for others but not themselves, and they shy away from answering simple questions like, "What restaurant should we go to?" or "What time should we leave?" A typical answer of theirs might be, "Oh, I don't care. Whatever you choose works." We know these are not life-changing questions, but the answers are offered up automatically through a filter that aims to please someone else or avoid conflict. Even with some of the most trivial decisions, we aren't giving ourselves the opportunity to pause and think about what we may want.

As homework, these clients are asked to be mindful of these exchanges and take the time to truly reflect on what they want and verbalize it. They nearly always report back on how uncomfortable this is, but starting simple and thinking about easy preferences like where to eat provides a starting point. Using someone else's questions is an easy method to gain small doses of self-awareness and begin this process.

In order to earn a bit of extra credit, I will also ask my clients to be mindful of how they respond to compliments from others. Often, they deflect compliments to ease the discomfort of being in the spotlight or respond with a remark that downplays the praise. Statements like, "It wasn't a big deal." or "No, you look great! Loving the new look." end up canceling out the space someone intended to create for them. This tendency misses the opportunity to accept a compliment, either by redirecting the attention or believing the praise is untrue or unnecessary. I challenge these clients to welcome the space rather than fear it or deflect. A simple "thank you" will often do.

Compliments, affirmations, and forms of validation should be seen as energy you can soak up rather than deflect. Soaking up the space that others create for you is not selfish. It is a way to refuel. When others make space for you, view this as another source to generate connection and manage exhaustion. This mindset shift helps you become more of a participant in the moment rather than occupying these spaces with underlying assumptions or worries.

Many of us have experienced or continue to experience symptoms associated with burnout or languishing. Burnout is marked by exhaustion and detachment from prolonged stress, while languishing is a sense of stagnation and indifference, lacking activation or joy. Constantly feeling energized isn't a realistic goal. Instead, a good place to start is by limiting distractions and avoiding multitasking when engaging in activities meant to be relaxing or enjoyable. Setting these boundaries helps you stay present and encourages a positive shift in your mindset. When this happens, you can fully experience the benefits of these moments.

Taking a walk, having a cup of tea, chatting with a good friend, or watching a show are all great examples of creating space for yourself to relax and unwind. It becomes counterproductive, though, when we fail to make an effort to shift our mindset and enter this space while distracted. Removing such distractions—for example, our devices—will help us move into the moment with more deliberation and presence. Have you ever checked your social media on your phone while watching a show on the sofa, only to realize you weren't fully present for either?

The thought of adding or removing a habit from your rhythm can be overwhelming. Does your mind have a tendency to create roadblocks or distractions? Perhaps it tries to subtly convince you that the efforts involved in making even a small change are just too daunting or are simply not worth it. Like many, you might find yourself leaning on the familiar refrain of being too busy to make a shift or incorporate something new. What if, instead of carving out extra time for yet another thing to do, you could simply harness the opportunities that already exist in your day?

Noticing When Your "Space" Is Full

If you are constantly operating with a sense of urgency or become easily overwhelmed, you are likely running at your capacity. You might feel too drained to even consider engaging in activities that could help you feel refreshed and reenergized.

Don't overthink it. Adjusting or letting go of certain things that take up space in your life can be simpler than you think. Be aware of how you transition and how you fill your time. Establishing clear boundaries begins by frequently checking in with yourself and saying no when you are at capacity. When we constantly push our limits, make assumptions, and place others' potential judgments or emotions ahead of our own, we lack the space and energy needed for self-rejuvenation.

When working with clients, I often ask them to pretend as if they had a balloon in their belly. This balloon fills with air throughout the day from stressors, responsibilities, and difficult interactions. Without being mindful of our energy output and finding ways to gradually release that buildup, we're bound to "pop." Sometimes it only takes a minor incident to push us over the edge. We're then left with the task of regrouping and putting the pieces back together. Finding proactive ways to release the pressure and reset can help us manage stress and energy more effectively.

Creating Space for Others

We can usually recognize the difference between interacting with someone who creates a safe space and someone who is distracted or judgmental. If we, as serial fixers, truly want to support others, we must learn to create that safe space. When it comes to people, multitasking is never productive. Creating a space for others that is safe requires presence, empathy, and patience. More often than not, people hear what someone says and immediately associate it with one of their experiences. Then they proceed to share that experience, which redirects the conversation and shifts the roles of the individuals involved.

We tend to falsely view relating as a form of validation, but this behavior can interrupt expression of vulnerability and diminish the interaction's safety. A self-disclosure like this is a great tool, but it needs to be done with the intention to build trust and quickly turn the conversation back to the other person.

One way to thoughtfully introduce a personal anecdote is to ask if they are able to answer a question or listen to something that has been on your mind. Their answer should give you a good indication of their availability before you share. These questions also give them the opportunity to assess their ability to redirect their attention in that moment and gracefully transition. They may ultimately realize that they do not have the space and need to find another time when they can be more present.

It's often said, "The wisest people don't need advice, and fools won't take it." As a space creator, your goal isn't to give good, effective advice (advice that others typically do not receive and successfully execute). Instead, ask questions that communicate curiosity and give the advice seeker an opportunity to process their thoughts and feelings. This also encourages them to assess what their options are and what they can control. We acquire confidence by gaining reps. The more we familiarize ourselves with an experience or practice a technique, the more we learn about it and ourselves in the process. As an athlete, I spent countless hours building muscle memory. Repeating certain drills or simply shooting free throws in my driveway helped increase my self-awareness and what worked best with my body. My confidence grew as I practiced and took risks in order to reevaluate and identify what I needed to work on next.

The mind works in a similar way when it comes to repetition and building confidence. Those raised by parents or caregivers who constantly solved problems for them and shielded them from discomfort missed out on critical opportunities—reps to stand up for themselves, ask a teacher for clarification, or navigate peer conflicts. Likewise, many of the children and teens I've worked with struggled to develop self-connection and confidence. They were often raised by parents who, despite their best intentions, lacked the energy, capacity, or knowledge to create a supportive space for growth.

Readjusting Your Physical Space

Life continually pushes us to adapt and adjust. We've all experienced countless moments that required us to reassess and reconfigure our routines. But when was the last time you truly examined the physical spaces you've created for yourself? Are they cluttered, barren, or soothing? These environments can be a direct reflection of your emotional state and significantly influence your level of motivation and well-being.

Take a moment to think about how you can improve your space. Consider changes that could evoke the feelings you want to experience more often and help clear your mental clutter. Maintaining mental wellness is like a dance, requiring us to work from the inside out and the outside in. The way we move through our day and the spaces we engage with have a profound effect on our thoughts and reactions. This process doesn't have to be complicated or require a major renovation. It could be as simple as opening the blinds, lighting a candle, reorganizing your workspace, or rearranging some furniture.

We are more sensitive than we realize to the energy we exchange with others and the atmosphere certain spaces create. Check in with your "balloon" and be mindful of the environments you occupy and the spaces you create for others. Some of us may need to take up more space and assert ourselves, while others might benefit from being more aware of how we show up and engage with those around us. Humans are not designed to "be on" at all times. Creating space to process all the information we consume is a healthy practice that shifts us into a more proactive state.

Make a habit of taking up space, but remain mindful of how it impacts those around you—others who are equally entitled to cultivate their own unique spaces. Balancing your presence with consideration for others is no small feat, especially when grappling with your inner dialogue. Do you have a love-hate relationship with your inner monologue? That voice can either fuel your ambition or paralyze you with doubt, shrinking you to feel smaller than you are. It often masquerades as protection, trying to shield you from shame, embarrassment, or failure. But when left unchecked, it transforms into a harsh critic, sabotaging your growth and keeping you stagnant. This unchecked critic doesn't just steal your confidence—it silences your curiosity and stifles the openness needed to navigate challenges, ultimately robbing you of your ability to fully engage with life's opportunities.

Your InnerCritic is constantly at work, pulling from past experiences while analyzing the present and scanning for potential threats. Unfortunately, it often operates through a negative, self-centered filter. The "what-ifs" rush in, making it hard to access resilience or problem-solving skills. You might become consumed by imagined judgments from others or paralyzed by the certainty of failure you've convinced yourself is inevitable. These spirals, fueled by perfectionistic mindsets, do more than undermine your confidence—they strengthen negative neural pathways, reinforcing patterns that make growth and adaptability feel even further out of reach. Left unchecked, the InnerCritic becomes less of a protector and more of a barrier, preventing you from stepping into your full potential.

There is good news, though. You are capable of creating new connections and positive associations in your brain. This process is called neuroplasticity. When you adopt a positive mindset that encourages positive self-talk, the brain changes and behavior modification can occur. First and foremost, change cannot take place without increasing your self-awareness. You cannot change what you do not know. Increasing your self-awareness is best done through regular check-ins.

Begin by allocating time throughout the day to:

Evaluate how you're feeling.
Identify the themes and commonalities of your thoughts.
Note how present you feel.
Monitor your InnerCritic.
Seek calm and focus.

These check-ins aren't about self-judgment or immediately trying to fix or eliminate uncomfortable emotions. Instead, they're an opportunity to validate what you're feeling, gather insight, and identify thought or behavioral patterns. Once you've done this, you can shift into rebalancing your emotions with logic and assessing your options. The goal is to decide whether the thought process deserves your attention and energy or if it's better left unattended.

Meet Nina

Nina contacted me seeking therapy in the midst of the COVID-19 pandemic. She shared that she was having trouble concentrating, and her anxiety had been higher than normal. She was in her mid-fifties and she and her husband had recently become empty nesters. It was evident after the intake session that Nina was a great space creator for others, but she neglected herself. She craved connection but often overinvolved herself in others' struggles, leaving little energy for her own care and challenges. Her relationship with her mother was strained. Her mother lived in near isolation, surrounded by piles of belongings and stacks of papers, a physical manifestation of the emotional distance between them.

Nina was sexually abused as a child. When Nina was a teen, she was dismissed by her mother when she told her what had been happening for years. Their already strained relationship fractured further, leading to long periods of estrangement. As her mother aged and required care, Nina—driven mostly by guilt—would make the hour and a half drive to help with groceries or clear just enough clutter to create safe walkways from the bedroom to the kitchen. She described these visits as both triggering and exhausting. Beyond creating physical space for her mother, Nina worked to cultivate emotional space, asking questions and offering advice on building connections and self-care. These efforts were met with resistance, resulting in no lasting changes or new routines.

Nina worried constantly—about her mother, her kids, her friends, her husband. At night, she lay awake, stewing over her weight gain and the unsettling realization that her current relationship with her boss mirrored one she'd experienced in her thirties. Her first business partner had been her best friend, which felt like a safe arrangement at the time. In that relationship, Nina took on the role of the "accommodator," convincing herself that her friend's strong personality and opinions were just part of who she was. Nina prided herself on being laid-back and able to get along with anyone.

Nina protected others by accommodating their needs to avoid conflicts or discomfort. While she often felt depleted, her InnerCritic justified this sacrifice by convincing her that her purpose was caretaking. Nina maintained vague boundaries, unaware that resentment was quietly building beneath the surface. Her business partner eventually overpowered her, taking control of the business and replacing her with someone else. She was left feeling confused and betrayed. These same emotions mirrored her strained relationship with her mother. The spaces Nina had historically created for others often worked against her because they failed to honor her own values and needs. She never set aside time to process her feelings. She noticed her thoughts but didn't acknowledge them. Running on empty had become her norm. Her body and mind, desperate for attention, began to send clear distress signals. She felt achy and prone to injury, battled nightly insomnia, and found her patience and focus slipping away. It was as though her body had taken over, forcing her to confront what she had long ignored: the need to declutter her life and reclaim her time.

Nina began to identify her patterns and consider the small steps necessary for behavioral change. The reps she needed for change to occur required a different kind of space that she was not used to creating. We started with addressing the basics. We identified ways to improve her sleep, increase her water intake, become a more mindful eater, and prioritize daily movement and exercise. We processed the guilt that came with these changes and addressed her feelings of unworthiness. She started small and used the tools we implemented to encourage structure without the rigidity. It was important for her to check in with herself and identify what her body and mind craved rather than blindly following a checklist.

As Nina progressed in her self-care journey, we examined the deep-rooted beliefs she had developed from a young age about feeling unworthy of care and attention. She reflected on how space was rarely created for her as a child, leaving her without the opportunity to develop the self-awareness and boundaries needed for a strong sense of self-worth. Although she faced moments of discouragement, her growing awareness and connection to herself became powerful tools to challenge destructive thought patterns and break free from self-sabotaging habits.

Nina shared that she feared an upcoming interaction with her mother and wondered if her mother would notice a change in her communication style and how she might react. Would she belittle her again? Use guilt as a way to reel her in? How would Nina stay on course and be more mindful of the space she was occupying and simultaneously protecting? Rather than entering the interaction without a plan, Nina would check in with herself and answer a series of questions:

What are the goals of the interaction?
Is there anything I want to get out of it?
Do I need to steer clear of a certain topic?
What signs do my mind and body generally give me when my boundaries are being compromised?
How can I end the conversation quickly if I need to?

Over time, Nina realized that sharing vulnerable personal information with her mother wasn't safe. To navigate their interactions more comfortably and avoid being triggered, she established a key boundary: *interact, don't engage*. This simple tagline served as a reminder to keep conversations light and neutral, focusing on safe, external topics like the weather or what she was planning to fix for dinner—subjects that required little vulnerability or unpredictability. When she was asked a question that could be incriminating, elicit guilt, or develop into an argument, Nina began to respond with validating statements ("Oh, uh-huh, that sounds like a lot. Is that so? What will you do next?") or paraphrase what she just heard ("It sounds like you were frustrated, so you told her this"). By approaching their interactions this way, Nina was able to create a sense of emotional safety for herself.

At one point, Nina wondered whether she should sever the relationship entirely, and we explored this deeply during one of our sessions. Human biology drives an intense desire to maintain some connection with our parents, even when those relationships are marked by trauma. When that connection is severed, we often find ourselves searching—sometimes desperately—for alternative sources of connection to fill the gaps or soothe the emotional wounds left behind.

Understanding her mother's tendencies and communication patterns left Nina feeling more prepared for their conversations. She could anticipate the requests and the guilt that followed any resistance, as well as the put-downs and subtle comparisons that used to leave her feeling exposed and drained after each interaction. Now, instead of being caught off guard, she was ready to respond with greater resilience.

Nina also came to realize that she didn't need to always be available. If she wasn't in the right headspace or was busy with other priorities, she no longer felt obligated to feed into the urgency her mother often imposed. I reminded her that the spaces she chose to occupy and create were ultimately within her control. For much of her life, those spaces had been dictated by guilt and a sense of obligation—accommodating others at the expense of her own needs. But Nina was learning to break that pattern and prioritize herself.

As Nina increased her self-awareness, she was able to carve out time for her mother on her own terms. She could prepare herself and review her boundaries before entering these interactions, which helped to lessen or prevent emotional hangovers. With practice, Nina found that the pressure began to ease as she gained greater control over the spaces she created for herself and the access she allowed her mother. She understood that establishing new boundaries might bring pushback or uncomfortable feelings from others—a natural reaction—but she was determined to persevere. Nina came to recognize that one of the key drivers of her ongoing anxiety was her lack of self-advocacy and clear boundaries. Acknowledging this was the first step toward reclaiming her peace and emotional well-being.

After several weeks, Nina seemed noticeably lighter. The constant internal chatter had begun to quiet. While her InnerCritic still lingered, vying for its usual share of mental "real estate," it was more balanced, thanks to her newfound awareness and coping strategies. She started applying similar boundaries to other relationships that had previously drained her energy and left her feeling off balance. Our therapy sessions shifted focus to the new emotional "space" she had created—and what she wanted to fill it with.

Transitions create opportunities for resets. In this case, Nina wanted to focus on creating space for herself and her own development and care. She now had the energy to execute a better sleep routine and incorporate more exercise into her week. Her confidence was growing, and she was dedicating more time and energy to connecting with herself. No longer overinvesting in others, she had freed up space to focus on her own needs and priorities. She could now genuinely show up, fully present and empathetic with others. Nina had reclaimed her values, along with a renewed sense of empowerment and control. Occasionally, in our sessions, she questioned whether this shift was selfish. Together, we unpacked this doubt, repeatedly confirming that it stemmed from false narratives crafted by her InnerCritic—an attempt to reclaim the space it had recently lost.

Creating Space for You

As we've learned, creating space for yourself begins with increasing your self-awareness and identifying behavior patterns. As our lives become increasingly fast-paced, many of us are losing touch with ourselves. The constant pull toward multitasking and the urge to fill moments of silence or stillness with stimulation have become deeply ingrained habits. Transitions throughout the day—those little interstitial moments, like waiting in line or walking to the car—were once natural opportunities for reflection, debriefing, or preparing for the next role. Now, they're often occupied by quick glances at our phones: checking emails, scrolling through social media, or catching up on notifications. While technology offers connection and convenience, its presence in these small moments can pull us further from our inner selves, making it harder to find balance and protect our mental health.

Instead of filling your transition times with fleeting, external sources of stimulation—like scrolling through your phone—try engaging with the world around you. Observe your environment, notice its details, and reflect on how your mind processes what you see. These moments, often overlooked, are opportunities to ground yourself and reconnect. When we default to our devices for structure or distraction, it's like consuming empty calories—briefly satisfying but ultimately unfulfilling. True rejuvenation comes from authentic, intentional actions that restore both your energy and your connection to yourself. By resisting the urge to multitask and intentionally framing certain activities as self-care, you can transform these small transitions into meaningful moments of presence and renewal.

Try This: Transition Pause

Identify a common transition in your life, like standing in line or getting the mail. Use this time to pause, take a deliberate breath, and notice something around you—the colors, sounds, or even the weather. Let this small moment help you reset and reconnect rather than reaching for a distraction.

As a space creator, it's essential to identify your nonnegotiables—the foundational tasks or efforts that act as your pillars. These are the practices that keep you grounded, provide a sense of accomplishment, and foster security and presence. While your days will inevitably bring unexpected challenges, maintaining a few certainties can help you feel more in control and steadily build your resilience.

Nonnegotiables are derived from and typically support your values. They help you honor who you are or want to be as an individual. If you are unsure of your values, perhaps start with the basics. Human beings require sleep, food, water, and movement. For many, these basic necessities are some of the biggest hurdles—especially for those who focus on serving, structuring, and solving for others while neglecting to extend the same care to themselves. This is where the journey must begin.

It is important for leaders, parents, or those in highly influential roles to monitor how well they are honoring their nonnegotiables. People around you are observing how you operate and what you prioritize. Living at an urgent pace, without leaving space for reflection or self-care, sends a harmful message about what is acceptable and sustainable and risks being emulated by others who admire or look up to you.

I have worked with countless clients who share a similar story. "I worked and fought for years, and eventually I depleted myself. I lost a sense of who I truly was and neglected the part of me that helped me feel whole, lively, and connected. The perfectionist in me pined for the glory, but I essentially kept creating new criteria once a previous set was achieved. I longed for others to validate me and view me as successful. I never truly took the time, though, to even define what the word *successful* meant to me. I repeatedly told myself that I would focus on my health soon, but it was all about productivity. I missed the part that maintaining my health was the very thing that would help me revitalize my motivation, feel alive rather than as if I'm going through the motions of life."

When to Protect Your Space Rather Than Create It for Others

Being a space creator does not require you to show up in the same way for every situation. Remember that boundaries exist for a reason: your protection. Interacting and engaging exist on a spectrum, with engagement representing a deeper and more vulnerable form of interaction. When you interact, you approach the exchange cautiously, evaluating the situation, gauging psychological safety, and assessing potential risks. This allows you to maintain a level of distance and self-protection, especially in situations where full vulnerability isn't appropriate or safe.

Engaging, on the other hand, involves a higher level of focus, presence, and emotional investment. It's about intentionally creating space for connection and allowing yourself to be more open and authentic. Both are valid and necessary, depending on the circumstances and the people involved. There are likely individuals in your life you encounter repeatedly—not necessarily by choice, but by circumstance or obligation. In these cases, you might choose to remain at the interaction level, keeping things light and guarded rather than moving into full engagement. Recognizing where someone belongs on this spectrum can help you protect your emotional energy while still maintaining necessary relationships.

Serial Fixers To-Do List for Creating More Space

Incorporate pauses. Schedule brief breaks throughout your day to check in with yourself. Use these pauses to breathe deeply, observe your surroundings, and assess your emotions.

Validate your emotions. When experiencing anger or anxious thoughts, acknowledge and label your emotions without self-criticism. Express how you feel using "I" statements (e.g., "I feel frustrated when . . .").

Minimize distractions and multitasking. Reduce distractions by focusing on one task at a time. Refrain from multitasking to enhance concentration and reduce stress.

Engage your senses. Throughout the day, take moments to engage your senses. Notice the sights, sounds, smells, textures, and tastes around you. This can ground you in the present moment and increase mindfulness.

Create boundaries. Establish clear boundaries to protect your emotional well-being, such as setting limits on work hours or prioritizing time for self-care that genuinely meets your needs.

Celebrate small wins. Recognize and celebrate your progress, regardless of its size. Acknowledge the positive changes contributing to your overall well-being.

Incorporating these practices into your daily routine can significantly improve your emotional resilience and overall well-being. By pausing to connect with yourself, validate your emotions, and set clear boundaries, you create a foundation for lasting inner peace. It's not about perfection but progress. Each small step you take toward mindfulness and self-awareness is a victory in itself.

Embrace these strategies and allow yourself the grace to grow and adapt. Over time, you'll find that the moments of anxiety and frustration become less overwhelming, and your ability to navigate life's challenges with calm and confidence will increase. The path to emotional well-being is ongoing, but with these tools at your disposal, you're well on your way to a more balanced and fulfilling life.

Part 3

Support, Don't Solve

In this section, we explore "Support, Don't Solve." This framework transcends professions and roles; its beauty lies in its accessibility—anyone striving to be a space creator and empower others can apply it. By following this five-step approach, you can avoid absorbing others' emotions, internalizing them, and falling into the burnout cycle. It helps keep your ego in check, makes your role with others less draining, and allows you to remain a supportive ally without overextending yourself.

Through practice, you'll learn to show up with reasonable expectations, creating a sense of sustainable comfort and control. Again, empowering both others and yourself requires energy, and without focusing on your own rejuvenation, it becomes unsustainable. As my mother always says, "And how long are you going to keep that up?"

As an athlete, I would go to great lengths to achieve any directive given to me, viewing it as both my focus and a measure of success. My coach provided the structure I needed, while I relied on grit, determination, and, most importantly, affirmation from my coach to meet each challenge. When basketball ended, I found myself searching for that same structure and sense of purpose beyond the court. The transition was difficult, and I quickly realized I needed far more practice in creating structure for myself.

Graduate school offered a surprising parallel. Much like my coach, my professors provided guidance and direction, but their approach was different. They didn't simply hand out answers or clear directives. Instead, they skillfully set the stage, presenting case examples with a blend of explanation and curiosity, always leaving room for questions. As internships progressed, I found myself in a role similar to a student athlete again—juggling multiple responsibilities, presenting cases, seeking advice, and working to master the frameworks they offered. These weren't quick fixes or shortcuts but tools that encouraged critical thinking and fostered confidence through experience. Little did we know we were building our own knowledge, gaining reps, and developing confidence as clinicians.

We were taught to slow down, to notice and name our emotions and thoughts as part of gaining self-awareness. This helped us become present, intentional listeners who could set internal boundaries, even in challenging conversations. Much like learning to pace myself during practice, I learned to focus on step one before rushing to step nine. This deliberate pacing, this resistance to urgency, reshaped how we engaged with clients. It reminded me of an essential truth I had only begun to uncover as an athlete: True support isn't about fixing and rushing to provide solutions—it's about creating the space for reps and growth.

So now I want to share this same transformative framework to you, so that you can create space for others and approach conversations as a supporter rather than a solver. This approach is especially useful in discussions that involve multiple steps and evoke emotions, where the dynamics can sometimes create or reveal underlying imbalances. Think of the classic group project in school: There's usually that one person who is highly invested in the assignment, and one who depends on the rest to pick up the slack. This dynamic plays out in the same way in our real-life relationships, with the more engaged party feeling overwhelmed and burdened by the extra responsibilities.

As you continue reading, I encourage you to keep an open mind. Implementing these five steps will take practice—like building any new skill, you'll need to get your reps in before they feel natural and fluid. Be patient with yourself, and stay mindful of what your InnerPleaser, InnerRescuer, and Inner-Critic might be trying to protect as you shift your focus to preserving your energy in relationships. By making this shift and approaching conversations with empathy, you can empower others while maintaining your own boundaries.

To start, we'll discuss the importance of validation and how it sets the tone before moving on to empathizing—a skill serial fixers already have plenty of practice with! Next, we'll delve into inquiring, where you lead with curiosity while sharing your thoughts and concerns. From there, we'll focus on motivating, using a strengths-based approach to encourage progress rather than stagnation. Finally, we'll explore how to reconnect, offering support without taking false ownership, so you can show up for others in a meaningful and healthy way.

How to Support, Don't Solve

Become a 'Space Creator'

Validate Empathize Inquire Motivate Reconnect

Chapter 9

Validation—Creating the Space

The first step in the "Support, Don't Solve" framework is validation, which is often mistakenly equated with agreement. But in reality, validation doesn't imply agreement. Instead, validation is about recognizing and acknowledging the emotions and words someone is expressing. This is your first step as a space creator. Start by working to silence the internal urges to interrupt, agree or disagree, or share your own experience. This takes a different type of energy and presence. Pay attention to their tone, choice of words, and nonverbal cues, especially during in-person conversations. Many of us have a tendency to listen while internally multitasking—a habit that can make genuine connection difficult, particularly when energy levels are low. That's why checking in regularly and setting boundaries is so essential. If you truly want to validate the people in your life, offering them your full, undivided attention is crucial.

Just as validation isn't agreement, validation is also not the same as affirmation. Affirming someone usually involves reinforcing their confidence. For example, you might say, "You've got this, you're great at presentations," which helps boost their self-esteem and provides a sense of security or encouragement. However, jumping to affirmation too quickly can inadvertently dismiss the person's struggles, making them feel as though their feelings are not fully acknowledged. Affirmations are often used to help quiet someone's InnerCritic, offering quick reassurance or motivational support that helps them feel capable in the moment. Affirmations should only come after genuine validation of their experience.

Validation serves a different purpose. It's about acknowledging and legitimizing someone's emotions or experiences without necessarily offering approval or solutions. For instance, you could validate a friend by saying, "I can see why you're frustrated after all the effort you put into this project." Here, you're not necessarily saying the frustration is warranted, but you're acknowledging the person's feelings. Validation requires you to recognize what the person is experiencing, regardless of whether you share their perspective or their feelings. It's about listening, being present, and holding space for what they're going through without judgment or the need to change it.

While affirmation often serves to build confidence by focusing on the positive, validation nurtures connection and empathy by accepting what is. Validation helps individuals feel seen and heard, which can be more grounding and sustaining in the long term, especially in emotionally charged situations. Where affirmation tends to motivate or reassure, validation provides the foundation for deeper emotional understanding and mutual respect. Both are valuable, but validation offers a space for emotional complexity, allowing people to feel accepted in their full range of experiences.

This first step in the process is perhaps the most important because it sets the tone. It reminds you of your role and allows you to enter these conversations with boundaries and confidence. Validation doesn't involve sharing your own experience, immediately relating, or giving advice. It does involve connecting and creating space. The other person is in the driver's seat, and you are there to guide. I have worked with countless leaders who feel drawn too quickly to provide guidance, share their personal story, or offer step-by-step advice. There is a time and place for advice, but when given too prematurely, it detracts from the learning and empowerment that can happen. Validation comes first, setting the stage for collaboration.

Your first task as the listener, when someone says, "Can I ask you for advice?" is to validate. Validation can come in many forms. It requires you to tame a judgment that was triggered by what you just heard, refrain from telling someone what they should do and just acknowledge that you understood the message and emotion that they were trying to communicate. This could be a nod, a smile, or maintaining eye contact. This could include a clarifying question or you paraphrasing what you just heard. Respond with curiosity.

Relating with others and sharing our stories is critical for building self-awareness, learning, and making decisions. The goal is to build connection and gain clarity, not fuel dependency. When we are not directly involved in a situation, it is easier to approach it with logic and separate the emotion. If we are directly impacted or involved in a situation, it is more of a challenge to set a boundary with ourselves or avoid getting pulled down an emotional, even catastrophizing, rabbit hole of thought.

You have likely been approached by a friend or colleague who has directly asked you for your advice on an emotionally charged situation where you could offer valuable support and make a significant impact. They might feel scattered and unorganized in their thoughts and are seeking for someone to help structure them or provide them with an answer so they can rid themselves from the burden and hopefully gain some relief. You have also likely watched someone you care about make decision after decision sabotaging their well-being.

As a leader, parent, mentor, or friend, you want to refrain from taking false ownership and instead be a supporter. You are on their timeline, which may test your patience, but this is not your journey. Your empathy or frustration might be triggered, but your control is limited. People learn best when they take ownership of their decisions, allowing their brains to create meaningful associations and catalog the emotions tied to their experiences. Don't take this away from them.

The most effective leaders I've worked with avoid making conversations about themselves. While the brain naturally makes connections to process and relate, these individuals resist the urge to interject too quickly, which usually disrupts the dynamic and flow of the conversation. Instead, they approach others with patience, empathy, and curiosity, refraining from centering on themselves. They keep their ego in check and don't tie their self-worth to delivering groundbreaking advice. It can help to imagine yourself at a crossroads: You can either turn right, engaging the impulse to redirect the conversation back to yourself and step into a fixer role, or turn left, pausing to create space and activating your listening skills to support others without taking false ownership or risking enmeshment and dependency. As you gain practice and grow as a space creator, you may find that you operate with a higher sense of calm overall. Without adding deliberate effort, you'll naturally increase the trust needed in relationships and in isolated conversations.

For parents, it can be tough to watch your child struggle with difficult emotions and challenges. The instinct to protect them is natural, as one of parenting's primary responsibilities is to provide safety. However, protection does not mean control. Stepping in to solve every problem might offer immediate relief, but it robs your child of the chance to build resilience and self-trust.

Another essential responsibility of parenting is fostering independence and helping your children become self-reliant adults. When you intervene to save them, you limit their ability to gain experience and build confidence. You've been a kid before and have solved these problems, but now it's time for them to take the lead. Resilience, problem-solving, and perseverance are developed through practice. Shielding your child from hardship might make you feel like a hands-on, good parent, but it ultimately fosters dependence. To break free from serial fixing as a parent, start by validating your child's emotions and meeting them where they are. Simple phrases like "I can see why this feels overwhelming" or "That sounds hard" help create psychological safety. This approach allows your child to feel seen and supported, giving them space to process their emotions rather than shutting down or relying on you to solve the issue.

Ask open-ended questions like, "What are your options?" or "How can I best support you?" to encourage self-awareness and ownership. Children and teens often feel intimidated when communicating with adults like teachers or coaches. Guide them to take action in these situations, allowing them to experience the discomfort of asking questions or sharing updates. The pace at which they navigate these challenges may differ from your own, and their progress might falter. Be patient, soothing your InnerCritic or InnerRescuer's urge to "save the day." Consequences will arise, and poor decisions may be made, especially with peers, but these moments offer valuable opportunities for growth, adjustment, and learning. Let them lead, be a supportive presence, and empower them to navigate these challenges independently.

In a culture that accepts constant distractions and multitasking, genuine listening has become increasingly rare. Our attention is fragmented, pulled in a thousand different directions by the relentless demands of work, relationships, and the happenings of the world. Devices beckon with notifications, tempting us to divide our attention and fragment our focus, further hindering genuine human interaction. We find ourselves constantly running from role to role, rarely pausing long enough to catch our breath or connect with those around us. We seek quick fixes, "Band-Aids," or substances to soothe and falsely provide hope that this is just a phase.

But do we truly listen? Do we truly connect? In our relentless pursuit of productivity and efficiency, many of us have lost sight of the profound beauty of simply being present with one another, of understanding and empathizing with the experiences of those around us. We're bombarded with information, opinions, and demands, leaving us drained and disoriented in a world that never seems to slow down. Amid the noise and chaos, however, there remains hope. In quiet moments of reflection and introspection, and by being more deliberate and mindful, we can reclaim the lost art of genuine listening—which goes hand in hand with validation.

Meet Claire and Micah

I worked with Claire and Micah for about six months. Like most couples, they struggled with communicating effectively and feeling heard. Both acknowledged that they were highly competitive and prone to defensiveness. These tendencies threatened their sense of cohesion and sabotaged their conversations. They would leave interactions unable to recall the initial purpose, knowing the issue would cyclically resurface but remain unresolved. After our initial session, I decided to approach their therapy with a refresher on validation, to help them feel more productive as a couple.

Emotions often ran high during our sessions, and it was clear that "winning" was the objective more times than not. These sessions challenged me as I had to maintain boundaries to avoid being sucked into a referee role or siding with one partner. In our second session, Claire and Micah arrived, clearly on edge from what I assumed was an intense car ride. They sat apart and exchanged brief, clipped greetings. I did a quick check-in and began paraphrasing what each of them shared. I explained the purpose of this technique and asked how it felt to hear their words reflected back.

Later in the session, Claire and Micah were ready to try it themselves. Claire shared how she felt, skillfully avoiding the word "you" to encourage Micah's presence rather than defensiveness. Micah's task was to relay what he heard her say. He relaxed his energy when I reminded him that he didn't need to agree or take blame—this exercise was about listening and reflecting. We switched roles and repeated the exercise, doing so many times over the next several months.

Their InnerCritics were fierce, constantly fighting for control. However, we reframed the challenge as a fight for the greater good of their relationship, not a battle between themselves. While it wasn't picture-perfect (and setting that expectation would be counterproductive) they gradually embraced the power of validation. They learned to create space and set boundaries when emotionally unprepared for intense conversation. Claire's self-awareness helped decrease her anxiety, while Micah began approaching conversations with the mindset that they were on the same team, working against a problem. This shift softened his approach, allowing him to create space for Claire, trusting she would attempt to reciprocate.

Creating Space for Connection

Validation is the essence of active listening—empathetically acknowledging someone's emotions and experiences. By making the effort to understand what others are trying to communicate, we lay the groundwork for deeper connections and richer relationships. Pretend that you are attempting to decode a message. The message is being communicated to you through words, facial expressions, and body language. This lens tends to soothe the ego and allows us to tap into the focus required in active listening.

Paraphrasing, the act of reflecting back what someone has said in your own words, is an effective tool supporting active listening. But it's more than just repeating; it's about capturing the substance and spirit of their message, including tone, emotions, and nonverbal cues. Paraphrasing acts as a bridge between hearing words and understanding intentions. It takes a certain level of focus and energy to create this space for others.

Premature Relating

As an active listener, refrain from interrupting or imposing your own agenda on the conversation. This can appear to be a method of effective relating, but timing is critical. Active listening involves creating space, interpreting meaning, staying fully present, and quieting your ego. The brain naturally decodes information by drawing from our own experiences and associations, which can be a helpful tool. In many cases, sharing our own related experiences encourages the speaker to continue sharing if they feel understood or if their experience is normalized. However, premature relating can disrupt the flow of energy, shifting the focus to the listener and redirecting the conversation away from the speaker's narrative.

We've discussed boundaries at length, but it's important to review them in this section. As a reminder, boundaries can serve as guides in conversations, ensuring that dialogue remains respectful and productive. Setting and maintaining them involves recognizing when to step back and honor the space of others. By creating a framework for respectful dialogue, boundaries lay the groundwork for authentic connection and mutual growth.

Many of us feel pressure to always be available, even when we're not in the right headspace or are already at our capacity. We push ourselves to green-light conversations out of a desire to please or a fear of disappointing others. As we've discussed, this behavior disrespects our own well-being, but it also undermines the quality of the conversation. We've all experienced the discomfort of talking to someone who is physically present but mentally elsewhere. Being mindful of when we are at capacity and recognizing when we need to reschedule conversations for a time when we can show up fully present and attentive is respectful to not only yourself, but to others as well.

Tips for Active Listening

Minimize distractions. Find a quiet and comfortable environment where you can focus without interruptions. Before entering a conversation, take a moment to center yourself and transition.

Practice active listening skills. Engage in active listening techniques, such as maintaining eye contact, paraphrasing, reflecting, and clarifying to demonstrate your understanding and encourage the speaker to elaborate on their thoughts and feelings.

Ask open-ended questions. Encourage the speaker to expand on their thoughts and feelings by asking open-ended questions that invite deeper exploration and reflection. Avoid questions that can be answered with a simple yes or no.

Show empathy and understanding. Validate the speaker's emotions and experiences by acknowledging their feelings and demonstrating empathy.

Suspend judgment. Approach the conversation with an open mind and suspend judgment about the speaker or their message. Avoid jumping to conclusions, interrupting, giving unsolicited advice, or formulating responses before fully understanding what the speaker is trying to convey.

The art of genuinely listening always stands out to other people. By practicing validation, paraphrasing, and boundary setting, we not only enhance our interpersonal relationships but also cultivate a deeper understanding of ourselves and others. True connection soothes and reminds us of the things in life that help us feel truly alive and present.

If you want to be a space creator in conversation, rather than just hearing the words, truly listen. Humans are innately wired to pick up on subtle cues in communication, thanks to mechanisms like mirror neurons, which help us understand others' emotions and intentions. Pay attention to tone, word choice, body language, and facial expressions. Do they align with what's being said, or is there a discrepancy? The good news is you already know how to do this; it's a skill rooted in our evolutionary need to detect social cues for survival. By intentionally tuning in, you can maintain presence, tap into empathy, and foster patience during the interaction.

Remember, a space creator rarely interrupts. This takes practice and can be challenging when someone is sharing something triggering or contradictory to your beliefs. Self-awareness can help you remain in the listener role, rather than immediately jumping in with a thought or relating a personal memory. It's natural to want to relate, but it can derail the conversation. In my therapy sessions, clients often share memories or experiences that remind me of my own. I may feel pulled to share even if it might augment their reflection, but my InnerCritic reminds me to stay in my role. This is their time. I've learned to write myself a note on paper in real time, validating the thought, setting a boundary, and reminding myself to process it later. This practice builds self-trust and keeps my inner parts calm, knowing I'll revisit the issue rather than suppress it.

Validation doesn't mean fixing or taking on others' emotions. The fixer waits for a pause to jump in with advice or a solution. But don't fear the pause. Use it as a moment for reflection or release. Emotional shifts often happen during pauses. This isn't your invitation to fix or defuse; it's confirmation that you've cultivated a safe space for someone to be vulnerable and explore deeper emotions. A comforting look may be enough to encourage them to continue.

Showing up as a space creator alters your motivations, helping you maintain focus and contain the emotional exchange. If your mind wanders toward fixing the problem, it will struggle to remain present and maintain boundaries. If your goal is to fix or solve, people will begin to rely on you for this role, creating a dynamic where they hand over their emotional load to you every time. This is not about being unavailable or unsupportive; rather, it's about avoiding overinvestment in others' issues, which can sometimes serve as a way to subconsciously avoid your own.

Codependency involves learned behaviors where people overinvest in others while neglecting their own needs, often because they want to help or fix others' emotions. This leads to blurred boundaries and a lack of self-care. Although these patterns reflect strengths like empathy and loyalty, the serial fixer's challenge is to balance these qualities with healthy boundaries.

Codependency is a frequent topic in therapy. One of my primary roles as a clinician is to create a safe space conducive to self-exploration and getting "unstuck." Validation is essential in this process, but overuse can perpetuate a client's need for external validation, fueling dependency and people-pleasing tendencies. It's common to discuss relationships in therapy, identifying strategies to improve communication or set boundaries. However, staying in this validation space too long leads to stagnation, limiting the client's ability to take ownership of their role and initiate change. Validation is essential in therapy and relationships, as it creates space for others to feel seen and heard. However, when relied on excessively, it fosters external dependence, where individuals seek reassurance from others rather than trusting their own internal voice.

A well-adjusted individual relies on internal validation as their foundation. They understand their triggers and have worked to reframe negative thought patterns, reducing self-defeating talk. While external validation can enhance their self-connection, it's not their primary source of support. Clients who grew up with a healthy balance of external validation and opportunities to develop self-connection often demonstrate greater resilience. In contrast, those who lacked validation in their upbringing may develop an urgent need for it from others, becoming overly reliant on external structures.

The cycle of overreliance on validation isn't just created by those seeking it; it also involves those who frequently offer it. Individuals who provide validation often do so out of empathy and a desire to help. However, serial fixers contribute to dependency by relying on their role as "fixers" or "rescuers" to feel good about themselves.

On either end, both individuals may struggle to cultivate their own sense of self-worth. The seeker might become overly reliant on external approval, while the provider risks neglecting their own needs in order to keep the other person feeling good. To break this cycle, each party must prioritize self-validation and establish healthy boundaries, ensuring that their worth is rooted in an internal sense of value rather than in the approval or reassurance they give or receive from others.

If someone hasn't developed the habit of internally validating themselves—acknowledging their own worth, emotions, and achievements—they may struggle to trust themselves. This lack of self-trust drives a need for continuous reassurance from others. External validation becomes a temporary fix, like a Band-Aid that doesn't address the deeper wound. Without strengthening self-trust, people will constantly look for the next compliment or external cue to feel "okay." True validation isn't about inflating someone's ego or playing a specific role in soothing them.

Effective validation offers support in a way that strengthens a person's capacity to self-soothe and self-affirm, rather than becoming a crutch that they lean on in every interaction. The goal is to help them develop the internal resources to handle their own emotions, so they're not continually seeking external reassurances to feel "good enough." When we validate with the intent to empower rather than simply soothe, we help people build resilience, reducing the risk of dependency on external feedback.

In therapy, I need to assess the goal of the disclosure. Is the client venting to receive validation that their actions are correct? Are they hoping to bond with me at someone else's expense? Remaining neutral in these situations usually supports the client's ego without fostering self-discovery or change. While validating someone's frustration generates empathy, remaining in that space too long may reflect my own need to please, rather than encouraging my client's growth.

So, how do we actually validate someone without creating that dependency? It can be as simple as acknowledging their feelings or experience. For example, saying, "It sounds like it's been a frustrating week" or "I can see how that situation would be really overwhelming for you" helps them feel understood without jumping in to solve their problem. Even nonverbal cues, like matching their tone of voice or showing empathy through facial expressions, can go a long way. A concerned look or a calm nod can make someone feel supported without needing to constantly seek more reassurance.

Here are some examples:

"I can see how that situation would be frustrating."
"It sounds like you've been through a lot."
"I can understand why you feel that way."
"That's a lot, tell me more."
"That must have been really tough for you."
"I hear you and I can imagine how that impacted you."
"It's understandable to feel that way given what you've described."

"Your perspective makes sense in this context."
"I appreciate you sharing that with me."
"It's clear that this is important to you."

Bonding at Others' Expense

Unfortunately, bonding at the expense of others is a common practice in families, workplaces, and friendships. Within families, discussing a relative's behavior can create divisions and deepen wedges, leading to a lack of understanding and empathy. In workplace settings, colleagues might gossip about a teammate's performance to bolster their own reputation, while friends may connect through shared criticism, using negative remarks to bond without exposing themselves to vulnerability. These topics often feel more inviting and safer because they allow individuals to sidestep deeper self-disclosure. However, this type of commiseration shifts the focus away from personal growth and diminishes the need for self-reflection. When I notice this happening, I encourage clients to reflect on the purpose of their conversations: Are they gaining new insights or setting boundaries, or are they simply seeking validation and affirmation, thus avoiding deeper self-exploration?

I've worked with clients who rely on a chorus of people for support, but these conversations often involve venting, bashing, and codependency. Their friends validate their emotions, fueling anger and reinforcing their sense of righteousness. They run to others for advice but rarely to space creators who help them process and gain insight. As a result, they feel stuck, unable to understand why their attempts to change their partner don't work. Their attempts at relationship change have been externalized—if their partner changes, they'll be happy. This dynamic of dependency and the need for validation will never secure the desired change. As the listener, it's crucial to recognize when conversations focus too much on others' deficits.

What is the goal? Is it to help someone gain insight, or to bond over shared frustrations? Without clarity, the conversation risks becoming a cycle of dependency, preventing growth.

Why Validation Matters

In this chapter, you've explored the essential role validation plays in fostering meaningful connections. Validation isn't about agreement or simply offering affirmation—it's about recognizing and legitimizing the emotions and experiences of others. This practice prevents you from assuming a solution-focused role or reinforcing a role as a serial fixer. Offering advice should only happen when asked for, and even then, it's important to ask thoughtful questions to ensure you meet the person where they are. As a space creator, you resist the instinct to interrupt, relate prematurely, or provide quick fixes, instead focusing on deep listening, effective paraphrasing, and maintaining healthy boundaries.

The practice of creating space for others extends beyond personal relationships, into professional settings, therapy, and self-development. By avoiding the traps of codependency and overreliance on external validation, you empower others to get their own reps in, helping them develop self-validation and resilience. As you strengthen these skills, you not only deepen your interpersonal connections but also contribute to a culture of genuine listening and empathy in a world often dominated by distractions and superficial interactions. Ultimately, becoming a skilled space creator allows you to nurture more authentic relationships while supporting others in their journey toward self-discovery and growth.

Chapter 10

Empathize—Deepening Connection

Empathy and sympathy are often used interchangeably, but they have distinct differences worth noting. Sympathy involves feeling pity or sorrow for someone else's misfortune. It's the reaction of saying "I'm sorry" or feeling a sense of relief that you're not in the same situation. Empathy, on the other hand, is about genuinely understanding and relating to another person's emotions. As the saying goes, empathy is "walking in someone else's shoes." You are making the effort to truly feel and or internally relate to how this person feels. It goes a step beyond just connecting and acknowledging, and involves trying to understand and share their emotional experience. This doesn't require that you've had the same experience yourself but that you can imagine and connect with their feelings and how those feelings impact them. Practicing empathy involves being patient, listening, and resisting the urge to cut the other person's role by immediately offering advice.

Over the years, I've occasionally received the same type of feedback from friends who knew me well: I don't share much about myself. The first time I heard this was in high school, from a close friend and teammate I'd known since first grade. At the time, I didn't think much of it, but I eventually realized it felt easier to listen to her drama than to share my own. Sometimes, I didn't feel truly heard, or I disliked the advice I received. I also carried a fear of judgment or burdening others with my problems. It felt safer to let others set the tone and remain in the "responder" role, rather than risk vulnerability.

I heard this again in my twenties and more in my thirties. I realized it was time for more reflection on the matter. I began to analyze myself in situations with friends, colleagues, and even my partner. Was I afraid to be vulnerable and share? Of course, this depended on the topic and the space that was created for me. My InnerPleaser tends to take the lead, but I also prioritize reflection and have a strong sense of who I am and what I value: my self-awareness and intrinsic connection with myself. I was gaining rep after rep in listening and asking thought-provoking follow-up questions but lacked the practice and confidence to share my own thoughts and feelings.

I began sharing casual updates or personal experiences, only to notice that the person I was talking with would quickly share a similar story or offer a suggestion to "fix" my situation. These responses didn't usually frustrate me, but they often shifted my focus. My InnerPleaser would kick in, and I'd naturally fall back into the listener role—a role I subconsciously welcomed because it felt familiar and comfortable. But what I truly needed in those moments was an empathetic response, one that allowed me to feel genuinely heard without judgment or the rush to provide a solution.

When we assume the listener role, our ego often engages as we process what's being said. We might start asking ourselves, "Can I relate to this?" "Has this happened to me?" and "How does this make me feel?" This shift in focus to our own experiences leads us to miss the full depth of what's being shared. Even when we let the speaker finish, we often pivot quickly to sharing our own story in an attempt to bond and relate. Our biases and experiences can influence how we empathize with others so we must be aware of these biases and approach each situation with an open mind. Brené Brown's work on empathy is particularly insightful, emphasizing that empathy involves not only understanding another person's experience but also connecting with the vulnerability involved in sharing. In her book *Dare to Lead* (2018), she reiterated the importance of listening without judgment and resisting the urge to immediately relate or impose our own values, which aligns closely with the principles of "Support, Don't Solve."

Daniel Goleman, in his book *Social Intelligence* (2006), identifies three types of empathy: cognitive empathy, emotional empathy, and empathetic concern. Cognitive empathy is the ability to understand another person's perspective. It involves entering a conversation with the intent to truly listen and create space for the other person's experience. This type of empathy requires patience and active engagement, allowing you to comprehend where someone else is coming from. Emotional empathy, on the other hand, involves physically feeling or sharing in another person's emotional experience. While it's not about experiencing their emotions as your own, it enables you to connect deeply with their feelings, often allowing them to sense your genuine understanding and support. Lastly, empathetic concern is the ability to interpret how someone feels and anticipate their needs or how you might assist them, even if they haven't explicitly communicated it. This form of empathy is a valuable skill and can make a profound difference in personal and professional relationships.

Empathy is a remarkable strength, but when unchecked, can sometimes lead to overextension. Jumping in too quickly to solve or fill gaps in communication may unintentionally disrupt the balance in relationships, depriving others of the opportunity to articulate their needs or build essential skills. Over time, this dynamic can leave empathetic individuals feeling drained, burnt out, or even resentful. For instance, many nonprofit leaders I've worked with embody deep empathy and a profound drive to serve. Yet their willingness to take on too much often comes at the cost of their own well-being, leaving them struggling to sustain the very passion that fuels their work. Empathy isn't limitless—it thrives when paired with intentional boundaries and mindful replenishment. Instead of rushing to provide solutions, consider slowing down to validate, empathize, and collaborate. Ask how you can best support, rather than assuming or overstepping.

Meet Michael

Michael woke up and began his work routine as usual, leaving early to avoid traffic and tackle a few items on his list before his team arrived. He was a confident leader and prided himself on his ability to connect with his teams over the years and empower others to work beyond their perceived potential. A new layer of stress weighed on Michael during his morning commute—today was his annual review. Things had been tense with his boss for months, and he mentally rehearsed the questions he planned to ask and strategies to keep his emotions in check. He was bracing himself for a less than stellar evaluation, but even so, he could feel his anticipation heightening with every passing minute.

When the meeting began, Michael's focus wavered as another person entered the room—human resources. His heart sank, and a wave of heat spread through his body. His boss greeted him with a detached, almost casual tone, followed by three devastating words: "You are fired." Michael's mind raced, and his body sent him into high alert, but he managed to stay composed and focused for the rest of the brief meeting.

Afterward, he called his wife, who reassured him that everything would work out. While he trusted her words, the sense of disappointment lingered. It wasn't just about losing his job—it was the confusion and the feeling of being misunderstood. Michael couldn't shake the realization that his perception of his role and contributions was starkly different from his boss's narrative.

He received a few texts from his team that conveyed their shock and anger after they heard the news. The only person Michael had directly relayed the news to was another leader in the company. They had cultivated a relationship with a strong foundation of trust, respect, and authenticity. They challenged each other but also knew when to validate and support. His text to her was simple. It said, "Good morning, I won't be at the meeting later today, I was fired." She did not respond immediately, but this was typical. Michael knew that she was in another meeting and made a point to disconnect from her devices to ensure that she could be fully present. He felt the vibration coming from his pocket and read the message she sent back: "How do you feel?"

Short and simple, yet incredibly effective. It created space. There were countless ways she could have responded, but her question came from a place of curiosity and allowed Michael to share at his own pace. She refrained from rushing to soothe his emotions with statements like, "Oh, screw them! You're better off" or "Don't worry, it'll all work out." By asking how he felt, she enabled him to process his emotions without taking false ownership of the situation. In the following days, she empathized by checking in with him thoughtfully and asking for permission to offer support. She offered small acts of kindness while respecting his pace, ensuring she didn't push him to talk before he was ready or make it about soothing her own worries. By taking on a few more household responsibilities—not in an overprotective, coddling way but to prevent overwhelming him with unnecessary stressors or tasks that could distract, derail, or trigger him—she fostered a supportive environment. This allowed him to be present as he navigated this change.

Acknowledge how challenging it can be to remain close to someone while leading with empathy without becoming engulfed by their emotions. Empathy in such situations requires setting boundaries with ourselves, ensuring we don't bombard the other person or impose our own agenda on their healing process. This balance takes practice; it's difficult to navigate our desire to help while avoiding pressure or control. Yet this approach allows us to lead with empathy, creating an environment where the other person feels safe to express themselves without feeling overwhelmed. Michael's inner circle fostered a safe space for him, enabling him to process, heal, and decide his next steps on his own terms.

Challenges of Empathy

Empathy, often described as the ability to understand and feel the emotions of others, is a true superpower. Practicing empathy allows people to connect on a deep and meaningful level. However, those with high levels of empathy often struggle with creating and maintaining healthy boundaries. Empathic individuals may find themselves swept up in the emotions and struggles of others, carrying them as if they were their own. This intense absorption can blur the line between supporting and solving, leaving little space to protect their own emotional well-being.

This is why it's essential to check in with yourself frequently and assess the size of your internal balloon:

Are you creating enough space for recovery?

Are your boundaries intact?

Are you supporting rather than solving?

To sustain empathy as a true strength, practicing self-awareness and creating intentional space for recovery is crucial. Empathy does not require you to take on everything; it asks only that you walk alongside others, supporting them without losing yourself in the process.

Meet Jordan

"I recognize that I am not practicing what I preach. Am I a doormat?" Jordan said in my office, his voice tinged with frustration and vulnerability. A dedicated mental health counselor in his late thirties, Jordan had always been known for his deep empathy and caring nature. He made it a point to be available for friends and clients, often going above and beyond to provide emotional support. However, this commitment took a significant toll on his mental health.

Jordan frequently took late-night calls from friends in crisis and stepped in to help overwhelmed colleagues manage their workloads, believing that being there for others was the only testament to his worth. Despite diligently practicing self-care through yoga, meditation, and exercise, he felt increasingly disconnected from his own emotions and needs. He checked all the boxes on paper, yet these activities left him feeling unfulfilled and emotionally drained.

As time went on, Jordan began to experience compassion fatigue, along with panic attacks triggered by the mounting pressure to maintain the facade of the "perfect" counselor and friend. Trapped in a cycle of serial fixing, he sought validation through contributions to others, believing his worth was tied to how much he could do for everyone else. This unhealthy pattern fostered imbalance in his relationships and led to feelings of resentment and isolation.

In our sessions, I worked with Jordan to help him recognize the unsustainable nature of his empathetic approach. Untangling the associations he had with empathy proved to be a challenging process. His InnerCritic was deeply entrenched, reluctant to relinquish its power and constantly whispering that prioritizing his own needs was selfish. We discussed the importance of setting boundaries, both with clients and in his personal life, and I guided Jordan in reframing his beliefs about empathy. I helped him understand that being supportive didn't have to come at the cost of his own well-being. Together, we explored practical strategies for asserting his needs, such as learning to say no and prioritizing self-care without guilt, gradually shifting his mindset to embrace a healthier, more balanced approach to empathy.

We identified ways to establish productive boundaries around his availability, creating specific times for work and personal life. We practiced communication techniques to help him express his limits without feeling selfish or anxious. Additionally, we focused on mindfulness exercises to help Jordan reconnect with his emotions, fostering self-awareness and emotional regulation.

Through this process, Jordan began to crave release and escape from his overwhelming obligations, recognizing these feelings as legitimate rather than signs of weakness. He learned to embrace moments of rest and solitude without self-criticism. With newfound tools and perspectives, Jordan started to reclaim his sense of self, understanding that leading with empathy didn't mean losing himself in the process. He was no longer just going through the motions of his self-care routines; he was fully engaged in each practice, truly reaping the benefits of every yoga class and meditation and waking up feeling rested in the morning. Ultimately, he discovered that by prioritizing his own well-being, he could show up more fully for others, which helped to quiet the demands of his InnerCritic while also satisfying the needs of the InnerPleaser and InnerRescuer within him.

In the "Support, Don't Solve" process, you use validation to first acknowledge the person's feelings and then employ empathy to connect more deeply with their experience. This approach ensures that you are not only affirming their feelings but also engaging with them on an emotional level, providing more meaningful support.

Start with validation. "I understand that this situation is really tough for you."

This step is imperative for demonstrating that you recognize and accept their emotions without judgment.

Follow with empathy. "I can imagine how frustrating it must be. It sounds like you're dealing with a lot right now."

This approach helps you to relate on an emotional level, showing that you genuinely care about their feelings.

By combining both validation and empathy, you can provide a comprehensive and supportive response that honors the person's emotional experience while fostering a deeper connection that prepares you for the next step in the process: inquire.

Chapter 11

Inquire—Leading with Curiosity

The third stage of the process, inquire, aims to ignite the space you have just generated by focusing on increasing the person's self-awareness and ownership of their current hurdle. This step is generally challenging for those eager to fix things, as they tend to slip into solving mode or attempt to defuse uncomfortable emotions. Leading with curiosity while refraining from judgment can be a difficult task, but with practice, you will begin to occupy the role of a space creator in emotionally driven conversations rather than being a fixer or solver.

One tactic that might be helpful is to start by asking the person what they need at this time or how you can support them. An effective prompt could be, "What would be most helpful for you right now: for me to listen, reflect, or advise?" This encourages them to articulate their needs. Do they need space to externally process, share an emotion, or have the presence of someone else as they feel what they are feeling? Are they longing for a different perspective or structure? Think of yourself as meeting this person where they are, but appropriately challenging them to think a bit deeper or assess their situation in a way that addresses the root of their stagnation or feeling of being overwhelmed. The goal is to maintain the space you have already created. Actively listen and view their responses and roadblocks as puzzle pieces. You are not meant to put the puzzle together for them but to act as a guide and motivator to help them access the clarity and connection to create their own masterpiece.

Be mindful of your responses, even when you think they might be helpful. I took a grief and loss course where the professor shared real cases from her private practice, which engaged the entire class. One of my classmates jokingly asked our professor how many boxes of Kleenex she went through in a month, given her specialization in grief. Her answer surprised us. She explained that she never offered her clients a tissue when they began to cry. Confused, we glanced around the room for validation from our peers. "Offering a tissue, in most cases, would be to soothe myself," she said. She explained that it could inadvertently signal an attempt to stifle or suppress their emotion—when, in fact, she viewed emotional expression as progress. Many of her clients had strong InnerPleasers and often apologized when they cried, worried about making her uncomfortable or burdening her with their emotions. Instead, she always kept a box of tissues within reach but only offered one if the client asked. To her, the space she created was sacred, and interrupting that moment, however well-intentioned, risked halting the work.

Refrain from quick responses like "you should" or "this is what you do." These reactions often overlook the emotional complexities of predicaments or hurdles, which can activate thought patterns or false narratives that hinder a person's progression and well-being. Instead, prioritize meeting people where they are, resisting the urge to fix their issues or redirect the conversation to yourself. Stay attentive to those who communicate passively or lack clarity in their requests, as they may hope you'll fill in the gaps and accommodate their needs. This is a pattern when the InnerPleaser takes up the majority of your mental space.

Filling in the gaps and allowing someone to skirt by encourages imbalance and positions you as a solver, not a supporter. This dynamic undermines ownership and prevents the other person from getting the necessary reps in to grow and take responsibility. One of the defining instincts of a serial fixer is to interpret passive or indirect statements as a call to action, often jumping straight into problem-solving mode. This tendency bypasses the opportunity to simply meet the other person where they are. For example, hearing a comment like "this room is always such a mess," a fixer might immediately begin tidying up or planning to reorganize the space, driven by a desire to alleviate the frustration they sense in the other person's voice.

However, this approach skips several necessary steps. By solving the problem preemptively, the fixer not only assumes responsibility but also denies the other person the chance to take ownership of their feelings and decide how to act. A more validating response, such as "it does seem messy all the time," acknowledges the observation without making assumptions or rushing to action.

This small but meaningful shift keeps the responsibility—and the choice—where it belongs: with the person who raised the issue. They can then choose whether to clean up, let it go, or directly ask for help. This approach fosters healthier dynamics, encouraging others to articulate their needs clearly rather than relying on unspoken cues to be interpreted.

By resisting the urge to fill in gaps or solve problems prematurely, you demonstrate both self-awareness and confidence. You also model an empowered stance: one that values your worthiness to be present and heard without overextending. Meeting others where they are creates balance, reduces resentment, and cultivates mutual respect in relationships.

Advice

We tend to feel honored when someone asks us, "Can I ask you for some advice?" We feel needed, and a wave of worthiness typically flows through us as we perk up and anxiously wait for the topic to be disclosed. Rarely do we turn down such a request because it strokes our egos and ignites our curiosity. We don't want to disappoint. The InnerPleaser in us wants to fix and come up with a solution to alleviate this person's distress, confusion, or pain. At this critical juncture as the listener, your response plays a key role in shaping the conversation. One option is to jump in, take the question at face value, and offer a solution. However, doing so can emotionally entangle you in the situation, creating a sense of false ownership or responsibility for the outcome. Instead, resist the urge to immediately provide an answer or fix the problem. Shift your focus to creating space for reflection, allowing the other person to engage in their own problem-solving process.

Here are some common responses that can trigger defensiveness: "you should," "you need to," and "why?"

Instead of saying something like "You need to just quit your job" or giving a straightforward yes or no to a question like "Should I quit my job?" respond with curiosity. Avoid taking the bait. Not only do you need more context, but the very nature of the question suggests that this person is grappling with internal conflict and seeking external validation or direction. Treat this as an opportunity to explore their thoughts and help them strengthen their own decision-making skills.

For example, you might ask, "What would it look like if you did quit? Or what's currently keeping you in this job?" These responses show you've heard and understood their question while encouraging them to reflect and provide more insight. Even if you're convinced they should have quit weeks ago, remember—they haven't. Now, imagine if you said, "Yes, quit your job," and things turned out horribly. Do you want to carry that responsibility? Their decision is shaped by unique associations, thresholds, and personal filters that are different from yours. By asking curious, open-ended questions, you help uncover those layers and empower them to navigate their choices with greater clarity.

Meet Isabella

Isabella was recently promoted and eager to take on a leadership role. She acknowledged that she liked to be in control and found it hard to transition from her professional role to her personal ones. Her marriage challenged her, and she had difficulty adjusting to her partner's tendency to flee from emotional conversations. Isabella craved resolution. If an argument ended abruptly, her anxiety would steadily build, making it difficult for her to communicate clearly or logically. This pattern often carried over into her work life. Now leading a team of two, Isabella was acutely aware that her boss was closely evaluating her leadership skills. Her frustration grew with one team member, Shawn, who consistently agreed to the tasks she assigned but often failed to follow through or delayed progress. Isabella would gently remind him, only to find herself stepping in to pick up the pieces and create the next to-do list for him. The cycle was exhausting. She was unintentionally taking on more work, and the emotional strain was beginning to take its toll.

I met with Isabella and initially created space for her to vent. She shared her frustrations and confusion around Shawn's ability to stay structured and deliver. I guided Isabella through the first two stages (validation and empathy) and began asking questions (inquire):

What are the ultimate goals of your role as it relates to Shawn?
What are his strengths?
What have you taken false ownership of and why?
Has Shawn experienced the "natural consequences" of not completing a task on time?
What are you trying to protect yourself from?
Are these patterns, or are your responses new?
What changes can you make in your delivery?
What can you let go of?

What new boundaries can you create?

How can you communicate these changes to your leader?

As we processed these questions and discussed her next one-on-one with Shawn, I could see Isabella's wheels turning. She paused and said, "Wow, I've been micromanaging, haven't I?" She was able to draw a parallel between her attempts to soothe her own triggers by projecting those onto Shawn, leaving him room to hesitate, stall, and avoid. Shawn had identified the setup, the pattern, and Isabella's leadership style. He realized that she would bail him out. He would repeatedly convince Isabella that he was trying hard and verbalize his excuses, but she would fix things and default to her own way of executing every time. She was carrying the emotional burden and the anxiety and sense of urgency, the very motivator he needed to structure himself to produce and execute.

Isabella entered her next one-on-one with Shawn with different goals and a new style. She had taken the time to analyze her patterns and take ownership of what was rightfully hers while beginning to let go of the rest. This meeting would help her understand how Shawn would respond to her boundaries and transfer of ownership. That day, she became a space creator. Instead of an agenda filled with to-dos and urgency, she approached the meeting with curiosity. She asked questions and communicated her intention to step back, supporting but not attempting to fix or solve.

Shawn responded by asking his own questions, leaving the conversation with increased clarity and motivation. He acknowledged the clear repercussions of missing deadlines or failing to relay information on time, understanding that it could jeopardize relationships with his coworkers and lead to uncomfortable conversations about his performance. I encouraged Isabella to be patient and resist the urge to intervene when she noticed a glitch or delay. This was Shawn's opportunity to rise to the challenge, and either way, she was collecting data to manage the situations and decrease her risk of burnout and fatigue.

While he faced a learning curve, Shawn eventually thrived with the autonomy. Isabella had her doubts about how long this would last, yet she processed her feelings and managed her urgency outside of their interactions. As her schedule opened up, she resisted the urge to fill it with distractions rooted in her childhood patterns of rescuing and pleasing, often sacrificing her own needs for connection. Learning to set boundaries was new for her, but she was gradually implementing them in her other relationships.

Her main source of burnout stemmed from overinvolvement in others' roles, emotions, and hurdles. By supporting rather than solving, she not only decreased her stress but also generated space for herself. She noticed her energy levels increasing, allowing her to care for herself at a higher, more productive level. Lunch, which had previously been an afterthought occurring simultaneously with checking her email, became a dedicated time away from her workspace. She began meeting with a nutritionist and stepped away from her work to honor her newly created nonnegotiables.

Shawn worked through the immediate surge of stress that accompanied the boundary shift, demonstrating his capabilities as communication between Isabella and Shawn improved. Their relationship transformed from one of stress and imbalance to a collaborative partnership. She recognized that her attempts to control Shawn's actions were fueled by her own unresolved anxieties. By shifting her approach to support rather than solve, Isabella was able to establish new boundaries and foster a more collaborative environment. Shawn responded positively to the increased responsibility and autonomy, leading to improved communication and a more balanced workload for Isabella.

It's critical to not only be aware of your potential judgements but also to refrain from allowing them to structure your responses. Gathering more information prevents you from operating solely from your experiences and frameworks. Creating space for others requires you to dig a little deeper, investigate, and "inquire." You will begin to notice that as you get your reps in, your questions will become more natural and do just as they should, allowing for introspection and enlightenment. People will leave the conversation with a sense of direction and ownership. By keeping your judgment contained, you can avoid shame.

On occasion, there will be cause for concern or an issue that compromises safety. An effective way to handle this is to use your "I" statements.

"I am concerned for your safety and hearing that leads me to believe that something needs to shift immediately. What do you think that might be? How can I support you with that?"

Many leaders and parents are faced with conversations that ignite fear and concern. While expressing your worries is essential, taking complete control or avoiding it altogether due to uncertainty about the next steps is not effective. Verbalizing your feelings is impactful, but your response must stem from a place of genuine care rather than judgment or self-protection driven by your ego. We are perceptive beings and can usually discern the underlying motivations of others during interactions.

Here Are a Few Questions to Help You Identify and Clarify Intentions:

Do they genuinely seem interested in helping me?
Are they simply going through the motions?
Are they seeking personal validation or an ego boost?
Are they seeking genuine connection or merely filling a role?
Do they have their own agenda or personal biases influencing their input?

Are they willing to listen and engage with your concerns, or are they focused on providing quick solutions?

Those who have a tendency to impose judgments on others' behaviors ("I would never do that. I can't believe you've let it get to this point.") tend to have impure motives. They like to engage in conversations that give them access to someone's hardships, struggles, or drama simply because it provides an opportunity to compare the scenario to their own life. This is a good indicator that their ego is craving validation. This is not what a space creator aims for. These thoughts, comparisons, or even moments of gratitude will surface internally, but a space creator takes a pause to assess and acknowledge that sharing such thoughts might be harmful or counterproductive to the person you are engaging with.

Placing yourself in a role that aims to fix and immediately soothe generates a great deal of pressure. It's common for leaders and parents to avoid engagement or convince themselves that checking in with someone is inconsequential. When we opt for a superficial interaction, it often doesn't indicate a lack of care; rather, it may signal that we feel ill-equipped to provide the necessary space or guidance to address what someone is experiencing. However, checking in with someone opens the door for meaningful connection and doesn't demand an immediate solution. By validating their feelings, expressing genuine concern, or simply offering your attention, you can create clarity and reinforce that they are seen and deserving of external support.

Grief takes many forms and often isolates those experiencing it. The pain, confusion, and fluctuating emotions can feel overwhelming and impossible to fix. But helping someone through grief doesn't require fixing it. By shifting your goal to creating space for them to be heard and validated, you can ease the pressure and redirect the energy in a more supportive way.

The situation may still feel intense, but this reframed approach makes the objectives clearer and more manageable. Regular check-ins and thoughtful questions show your awareness and care, which can have a profound impact. With this perspective, offering support becomes less intimidating, less exhausting, and less emotionally draining.

Effective Inquiry Questions

Start by asking the person what they need at this time or how you can support them. Here are some questions to consider and add your own flavor to:

"What do you need most in this moment?"
"Do you need space to process your thoughts and emotions?"
"Are you looking for a different perspective or structure?"
"How can I best support you right now?"

Think of yourself as meeting this person where they are but appropriately challenging them to think deeper or assess their situation in a way that addresses the root of their stagnation or sources leading to feeling overwhelmed. The goal is to maintain the space you have already created and keep the ownership with them.

Common Pitfalls

Be mindful of common mistakes, such as:

Jumping to solutions: Avoid providing answers or fixes too quickly.
Inserting personal emotions: Refrain from letting your own feelings influence the inquiry.

Making assumptions: Ensure you are not assuming what the person needs or feels. Let them get their reps in and structure you.

Emotional Impact

Effective inquiry not only supports the person being helped but also impacts the supporter. By allowing others to take ownership and work through their challenges, supporters often experience a reduction in their own stress and a more balanced relationship dynamic.

Actionable Steps

Ask open-ended questions: Use questions that encourage the person to explore their thoughts and feelings.
Listen actively: Pay close attention to their responses without interrupting or offering solutions.
Reflect and summarize: Paraphrase what you've heard to confirm understanding and validate their experience.
Encourage Self-Reflection: Prompt the person to consider what changes they might make and how they can achieve their goals.

Reflection Prompts

To evaluate your practice of the inquire stage, consider the following:

How often do I find myself slipping into fixer mode?
What strategies can I use to stay in a space creator role?
How does my approach impact the person I'm supporting and our relationship?

Creating space for others involves not only asking the right questions but also avoiding quick fixes and judgments. The inquire stage is about fostering self-awareness and ownership, which ultimately leads to more meaningful growth and understanding. By practicing effective inquiry, you enhance your ability to support others while also protecting your own well-being.

Chapter 12

Motivate—Fueling Strength

Motivating others without taking false ownership of their problems involves striking a balance between providing genuine support and fostering their independence. True motivation empowers others to grow, make decisions, and take responsibility for their challenges—without you stepping in to "save" them. While many of us derive a sense of purpose and validation from helping others, this urge to nurture must be paired with boundaries that allow space for personal reflection and growth, both for yourself and those you aim to support.

Motivation, at its core, is not about fixing; it's about encouraging and inspiring others to find their own path forward. This means resisting the urge to overstep, solve problems for them, or absorb their struggles as your own. Instead, it's about asking thoughtful questions, highlighting their strengths, and guiding them to discover solutions they can own. By doing so, you not only respect their autonomy but also conserve your energy for the internal work that fuels your ability to truly be present for others. This approach creates a sustainable cycle of support that uplifts others while keeping you grounded.

Self-Check-In Before You Begin

The next step in the "Support, Don't Solve" model is to motivate. This step requires mastery over time, as it involves finding a delicate balance between offering support and encouraging self-reliance. To pinpoint where motivation belongs in your interactions, reflect on how open and ready they were during the "inquire" step. Were they guarded or still overwhelmed? Are you moving to the next stage for your benefit, or are you genuinely maintaining your role as a space creator? You can refine your process through patience and reps as you build your ability to read both verbal and nonverbal cues.

Recognize that every person you interact with—no matter the depth or length of the relationship—has been shaped by their own unique journey. Their experiences, especially those from childhood, have likely influenced how they perceive themselves and respond to challenges. For those raised in environments marked by apprehension and anxiety, altering their InnerCritic can be particularly difficult. This voice often mirrors the dismissive remarks they grew up hearing, such as "You'll be fine," "Stop worrying," or "It's not that bad, move on." These quick attempts to avoid uncomfortable emotions may have undermined their sense of worthiness and left them feeling invalidated.

Without the tools to self-validate, they may continue seeking approval or guidance from individuals who replicate the dynamics of their past. As a space creator, you have the opportunity to break this cycle by modeling a different way. Through genuine presence, validation, and thoughtful engagement, you can help them experience what it feels like to be seen, heard, and valued without judgment. This shift can create powerful moments of connection and foster the growth they may not yet believe is possible.

It's like the old saying goes, "Give a man a fish and you feed him for a day. Teach a man to fish and you feed him for a lifetime." (This applies to women too!) Providing the space for someone to access clarity and gain reps sometimes requires a push or encouraging statement. This step is the defining line between engrossing yourself in someone else's predicament (false ownership) or maintaining a supportive, structuring role.

When motivating others, it's important to focus on what they need and want, not what you would do or desire in the situation. Focus on highlighting their strengths, abilities, and past successes. Remind them of their potential and the positive impact they can make. Help them recognize their progress and growth, celebrating even the small victories along the way. By doing so, you foster a sense of confidence and self-belief, encouraging them to face challenges head-on without feeling the need to rely on external validation or ego stroking.

Motivating others takes many forms and begins with understanding what resonates with each individual. As a leader, investing time to learn your team members' learning styles and how they best receive praise and validation can make a significant difference. For some, motivation stems from consistency and genuine curiosity about their evolution. For others, it's the recognition of steps they've already taken and acknowledgment of their efforts, even when the path feels challenging.

Using a **strengths-based approach** helps redirect focus from self-criticism to constructive reflection. This doesn't mean dismissing pain or invalidating struggles by glossing over them with positivity. The goal isn't to "fix" or prematurely shelve difficulties but to highlight progress—even small victories—that can build momentum. By focusing on efforts and shifts, however subtle, you can help spark forward movement and gently

> **strengths-based approach**—Identifying and emphasizing the positive aspects or strengths in someone's behaviors or thoughts. This approach focuses on recognizing and building upon what is working well to foster growth and resilience. The goal is to challenge any negative associations someone may hold about their thoughts and behaviors or to empower them to reframe their perspective and approach their situation with confidence.

challenge a mindset that has kept them stuck. This approach fosters resilience and shows that growth is possible, even in the face of adversity.

These Types of Questions Can Help with Clarity and Spark Motivation:

"What are your biggest takeaways?"
"What do you identify as the next step?"
"What do you hope to learn?"
"What feeling or thought do you need to find closure with?"
"How can you validate or acknowledge yourself?"
"You're on a mission; how can you fight back?"

These clarifying yet strengths-based questions not only confirm that you are on their team but also that you believe in their ability to shift. There is no urgency or pressure interwoven in these statements, but their goal is simply to awaken a growth mindset or perhaps give them a jolt of motivation. Highlighting past hardships they have navigated helps them acknowledge some of their abilities and tap into their resilience bank. This is another attempt to challenge negative thoughts and combat stagnation or feeling overwhelmed.

A space creator aims to allow others to be their authentic selves and tap into their vulnerability—not for their own sake but for the sake of people they care about. If a high level of trust is present, don't be afraid to hold people accountable and challenge their conflicting responses and behavior shifts. This requires you to pay attention and take mental notes of how someone operates. Before giving feedback or confronting someone as a means to challenge a misalignment in their thinking or behavior, receive permission first:

"Can I give you some feedback?"
"I've noticed something that doesn't seem to add up; can I share?"
"I am confused by this; can I hear your thoughts?"

A space creator is able to uncover the true essence of someone's motivations, resilience, and strengths. The ability to simultaneously validate tough emotions and help someone reconnect with their inner power is an art form. One that can be acquired with reps and the awareness it takes to create effective, safe spaces for others and yourself.

This description might remind you of a coach. The best coach I ever had the privilege of playing for was tough on me, but her words were spoken in a way that radiated faith. I trusted her and knew that her words, even when they were harsh and critical, came from a positive place. Her intentions were to push me and make me the best version of myself on the court and off. She acknowledged where I was but helped me balance out my own negativity and challenge my InnerCritic. She identified that my InnerCritic was a major obstacle. My perfectionism could serve as a motivator in some situations, but ultimately it triggered fear, self-doubt, and stagnation.

It's crucial to foster a sense of autonomy and ownership in the individuals you choose to motivate. Encourage them to identify their own goals, aspirations, and the steps needed to achieve them. By empowering them to take control of their own journey, you allow them to develop a genuine sense of responsibility and motivation. Offer guidance and support when necessary but always with the understanding that the ultimate decision-making lies in their hands.

Parents often strive to raise confident, self-sufficient adults, motivated by a deep love and a desire to give their children the best possible foundation. However, this well-intentioned goal can inadvertently go astray when parents focus too much on protecting their children from challenges, uncomfortable emotions, or tough decisions. By shielding them, parents risk depriving their children of the essential "reps" needed to develop critical life skills—like problem-solving, emotional regulation, and resilience. These are not just nice-to-haves; they are the cornerstones of adulthood, equipping children to navigate an unpredictable and often demanding world.

Encouraging children to face challenges early, process their emotions, and weigh options fosters a deeper sense of self-awareness and confidence. When kids are allowed to stumble, reflect, and try again, they begin to see themselves as capable decision-makers. They learn that discomfort and failure are not signs of inadequacy but natural parts of growth. Over time, this builds a resilience bank they can draw from in the future—a well of confidence and adaptability that prepares them for life's inevitable curveballs.

Moreover, allowing children to practice these skills reinforces the importance of personal care and self-prioritization. They start to see how their choices shape their outcomes and begin to internalize the value of creating structures that support their own growth and well-being. This approach not only helps children thrive in the present but also lays the groundwork for them to become adults who can stand firmly in their independence and navigate the complexities of relationships, careers, and personal goals with grace.

When parents step back, provide guidance without overstepping, and allow their children to experience natural consequences, they empower them. This empowerment isn't just about raising resilient kids—it's about raising adults who believe in their ability to face challenges, care for themselves, and chart their own paths.

The human filter—the ability to evaluate and sift through the advice of others—prevents you from being overly accommodating and empowers you to live on your own terms. People offer suggestions based on their experiences, which may not align with your circumstances. The effectiveness of their advice depends on your specific situation and the barriers you face. Learning to filter advice is vital for accessing your beliefs and fostering autonomy. You'll find some advice isn't useful to you. Avoid becoming dependent on others for decision-making. True autonomy comes from considering various viewpoints while trusting your own judgment. Consider advice that aligns with your values and goals, empowering you to maintain control over your choices and individuality while benefiting from the wisdom of others.

Motivating others without assuming false ownership is a nuanced practice that requires empathy, self-awareness, and the ability to create space for growth. By fostering a supportive environment, serial fixers begin to empower individuals to take ownership while developing their resilience and autonomy. As leaders and parents, we must resist the urge to fix, as this tendency can lead to burnout and hinder genuine progress for both ourselves and those we aim to support. Embrace the art of questioning, validate emotions, and celebrate small victories to encourage confidence and self-belief in others, which brings us to the final stage: reconnect.

Chapter 13

Reconnect—Maintaining Support

You've arrived! You're now exploring the final stage of the "Support, Don't Solve" framework: reconnect. This step emphasizes sustained support and solidifying the connection that was built during earlier stages. Reconnecting after a conversation—or a series of conversations—demonstrates ongoing interest and care. This might be as simple as sending a text, writing a card, or stopping by someone's desk or home to check in.

Think of a time when you shared something vulnerable with a friend, asking for help in navigating a difficult, emotional situation, and they followed up later to ask how you were doing. It felt good, didn't it? It confirmed you weren't alone and that someone was making an effort to support you through something hard. That's the essence of reconnect.

Reconnection is not a one-size-fits-all effort. It takes on different forms depending on the relationship and circumstances. Whether it's a quick text or a more involved conversation, the goal is to demonstrate authentic care and concern. It shows that the person is worthy of your time, thought, and energy—even after the initial moment of vulnerability has passed.

This process of checking in also communicates trust in their ability to manage their situation and process their emotions, with you providing the space they need. You are not solving; you are supporting and encouraging their growth.

Meet Adele

Adele was in her senior year of college and had been best friends with Olivia since their freshman year. The two young women were inseparable. They were in the same sorority and shared the same major. Olivia began dating Matt at the end of their junior year and her time naturally shifted away as she spent more time with him. Adele was happy for Olivia and wanted to support her as her relationship with Matt progressed. He seemed like a nice enough guy, right? Olivia said she was happy—most of the time. Still, Adele couldn't completely ignore the subtle, nagging unease she felt when Matt was around. Over the next six months, Adele found herself consoling her best friend more and more after weekends spent with him.

Olivia, who had left her history of sexual abuse mostly unaddressed, now found it surfacing in nearly every conversation. She revealed to Adele that she had been raped by her high school boyfriend, something she thought she had left in the past. At the start of her relationship with Matt, sex had been fun and fulfilling, but now it triggered flashbacks to her trauma. During intimacy, Olivia often froze or shut down, embarrassed and confused by her reactions. She didn't want Matt to feel insecure or rejected, so she would push through—but it was becoming harder each time. The effects were spilling into other parts of her life. Olivia began experiencing nightmares and noticed growing anxiety throughout her days. She couldn't understand why these reactions were emerging now. Freshman year, she'd had more casual hookups, and those never felt this way. Why now when she was in a committed, safe relationship? Why was her body reacting as if she weren't safe at all? The questions haunted her, layering confusion and guilt onto the anxiety she was already battling. Olivia was desperate to make sense of what she was experiencing but felt trapped, uncertain about how to address it without unraveling her relationship.

Matt's frustration with the situation grew, no matter how many times Olivia reassured him that it wasn't his fault. Adele, once accustomed to hearing laughter through Olivia's bedroom door, now heard Matt yelling instead. The warmth and joy that had once filled their relationship had evaporated. Adele spent countless afternoons consoling Olivia, urging her to leave. "He's an ass. I hear the way he talks to you. What you're going through is serious, and he's making it worse. You need to break up with him!" she would say, her voice full of both concern and exasperation. Through her tears, Olivia would agree with Adele's logic, nodding as if she understood. Yet she never took action. As the cycle continued, Adele's desperation to help her friend grew. Watching Olivia suffer while Matt continued to show up day after day left her feeling helpless and increasingly frustrated. She wanted to shake Olivia free from the grip of the toxic relationship but struggled to find a way to truly get through to her.

Adele and I began analyzing her approach and she processed her concern for her best friend and how it was impacting her. "I'm exhausted. I miss my friend. Why can't she see what's happening and move on?" We identified the role that Adele played in this scenario and how she was operating with a sense of urgency. Her efforts were actually perpetuating the cycle and she had emotional stock in the situation. I asked Adele to answer four questions to reveal structure and clarity in another way.

What can you control?
What are your options?
What can you let go of?
What is your role?

I also ask these questions when working with clients suffering from anxiety. These questions are grounded in logic, engaging the frontal lobe and prompting a shift in focus. By introducing logical thoughts, our emotions are essentially required to "make space," interrupting their intensity and reducing the tendency to ruminate. This solution-focused technique becomes especially effective once we've taken the time to identify and validate our feelings, creating a balanced pathway to both acknowledgment and resolution.

Adele answered these questions, and I encouraged her to verbalize all of the options she could think of, even if they did not align with her values and empathy. She chuckled at a few that were powered solely by her anger with Matt, but she began to understand how altering her approach would alleviate her and challenge Olivia. New boundaries were needed; ones that still embodied empathy and were designed to support her best friend.

As I entered the waiting room two weeks later to greet Adele for our session, I quickly observed that she was eager to get started and share some updates.

Adele began by sharing that Matt and Olivia had a huge fight about a week ago, leaving Olivia inconsolable after he slammed the door and left. Adele held her as she cried, and once again, Olivia asked what she should do, expressing her guilt and confusion. She repeated the rhetorical questions, turning to Adele for answers: "Why is sex different now? What is wrong with me? I am broken. Will I ever have a healthy relationship again?" Rather than trying to soothe Olivia by answering her questions or attempting to convince her—yet again—that she would get through this if she just tried harder (or break up with Matt for good), Adele decided to approach the situation as a space creator instead.

She went on to tell me that she started with validation and paraphrased what she had heard. Then Adele asked Olivia what was keeping her in the relationship and what needs were not being met. She also asked her to name her options. Adele remembered that her role was to support her friend with these questions and create a space for her to process the issues in a different way this time.

Adele shared that she ended their conversation by setting a healthy boundary, shifting into a role of support rather than problem-solving. Instead of offering Olivia endless options and responses—which often left her stuck in the same place—Adele took a step back. Like any new boundary, this created a shift in their relationship. Things between them remained cordial over the next several days, but Adele noticed that Olivia began keeping to herself and no longer made her nightly visits to vent and share updates about Matt.

Despite preparing for the awkwardness in therapy, it was uncomfortable for Adele. She was still able to self-soothe and remain patient and refrained from acting impulsively or slipping back into the fixer role. Later in the week, Adele made an intentional effort to reconnect. During their usual Thursday Starbucks run, she focused on reestablishing their bond by catching up on other areas of their lives. The conversation was resonating with balanced, healthy energy.

When the time felt right, Adele gently asked, "How are you and Matt? Any updates?" Her tone reaffirmed that she cared about Olivia's well-being and was open to discussing the relationship if Olivia needed to.

Olivia gave a small smile and replied, "Thanks for asking. That means a lot. I've been thinking about some of our earlier conversations this week and know I need to do something different. I'm just still figuring out what that is."

Adele nodded empathetically. "I know it's been a roller-coaster ride of emotions, but it sounds like you're on a good path toward making some changes." Her words conveyed support while also making it clear that she was committed to staying in a supportive role without taking emotional responsibility for the situation.

By maintaining this boundary, Adele protected her own well-being and helped break the codependent dynamic they had previously fallen into. Olivia seemed encouraged by her friend's validation, and a new wave of confidence washed over her. She realized the next step was hers to take—but also that she didn't have to navigate it completely alone.

Adele's shift in approach exemplifies the power of stepping back from the urge to fix and instead creating space for deeper reflection. This is where we often find ourselves as serial fixers, leaders, friends, and family members: resisting the temptation to provide immediate solutions and instead asking thoughtful questions that promote deeper exploration. By allowing Olivia to process her emotions and encouraging her to explore her own options, Adele not only supported her friend more effectively but also set a healthy boundary, which included consistency in their interactions.

Through this process, Adele effectively and consistently reconnected with Olivia on a deeper level, fostering an environment of trust and openness. This shift—from problem solver to space creator—can feel challenging, especially when we care deeply about the other person's well-being. Yet it's a critical step toward fostering genuine growth and empowering others to make their own decisions and get their reps in. By prioritizing connection over correction, Adele laid the groundwork for Olivia to find her path forward, demonstrating the profound impact of genuine support and the importance of maintaining healthy boundaries in any relationship.

The goal when reconnecting is to leave room for creativity. It could be as simple as a text, call, or in-person conversation that starts with checking in on this person:

"Hey, I have been thinking about you after our conversation and wanted to check in."

"How are things going? Are there any updates?"

"How have you been feeling? Is there anything I can support you with?"

These check-ins not only shows that you care but can, in many cases, communicate your faith in their ability to further process their issue and progress. It is theirs to own, but you are there to support and provide space if needed.

The responses to your connection or circle back may vary, but asking open-ended questions encourages them to reflect and reenter the safe space that you previously created. Sometimes reconnection will be short and concise; others may require more time, so be mindful of when and how you enter this stage and if your energy and schedule allow you to be present and step into your role as a space creator. Take a moment to check in with yourself and assess the situation using your intuition and emotional intelligence. Consider when to touch base and determine what form might be best received and most productive.

The most effective leaders I've worked with over the years have a keen sense of those around them and can identify behavioral shifts. This perceptive quality encourages regular check-ins, but it also prevents them from neglecting or forgetting to circle back after conversations that involve emotion. The trust and belonging that can be cultivated from such a simple effort are rewarding for both parties and directly impact the culture of a team or organization.

Sharing requires vulnerability. People will take risks when they feel safe and can trust someone to honor where they are and demonstrate that they truly care. The reconnection solidifies this trust and confirms that you were previously paying attention and reinforces your role as the space creator. People also tend to feel worthy when someone circles back to them in a nonjudgmental way. It fosters a relationship that feels fluid and authentic, rather than fragmented or fleeting.

The information that others share when you circle back should inform how you react. Do you need to revisit the options you identified in prior conversations? Or maybe you can celebrate and affirm progress or a mood shift. Things may or may not have changed significantly, but acknowledging the other person's effort and strengths remains an important part of the process. The goal is to empower them by recognizing even the smallest steps they've taken. This strengths-based approach is a powerful tool that influences mindset and motivation. It validates reps or possibly the strength it has required to persevere through difficult situations.

I have worked with many clients who categorized themselves as "stuck." They struggled to recognize their own strengths, often burying their abilities under layers of self-doubt and negative self-talk. Highlighting even a small effort—like the energy it took to show up for the session—could create a powerful opportunity for a mindset shift. As leaders, friends, or parents, referring to a strengths-based approach in the reconnect stage highlights and elevates the person's efforts. This step aims to help in confidence building, reframes self-doubt, and encourages action rather than passivity. Reconnecting can bring unexpected benefits and value, often in ways that are hard to predict. Even when someone says they're fine, their nonverbal cues or actions may tell a different story. Your role is limited to responding to the cues you observe from the person you're supporting. If your efforts aren't welcomed or acknowledged, it may be a signal to shift your focus inward—prioritizing your own path toward peace, letting go, and finding closure on your terms. It's their journey.

You might feel tempted to dwell on the situation and analyze it repeatedly, neglecting the fact that it is not your role to make adjustments and continue the work. This is an example of false ownership, where you could end up investing considerable effort in resolving something on your own and in isolation.

Space creators aim to simplify and bring clarity. They focus on identifying their role in conversations or situations, striving for authentic connection without carrying the emotional baggage of others. By creating space to support and lead with empathy, they avoid the trap of becoming the solver—resisting the urge to take false ownership in an effort to affirm their relationships, roles, or sense of worth.

In becoming a space creator, strike a balance between offering genuine support and maintaining healthy boundaries for yourself. This framework doesn't call for emotional detachment; rather, it requires an elevated level of emotional intelligence and self-awareness. As you pause to reflect on your role in each conversation, you begin to understand when to step in and when to step back. Reconnection reinforces your commitment to the relationship, allowing the other person to know that they really matter. It's a powerful way to show care without overstepping or taking on unnecessary burdens. This process also involves reframing how you view progress—shifting away from measuring success based solely on outcomes and toward valuing small efforts, resilience, and the courage it takes for others to confront their challenges. By highlighting these strengths, you empower those around you to take ownership of their process while freeing yourself from serial fixing and the emotional toll of trying to solve problems that are not yours.

Key Takeaways for Reconnecting

Pausing for reflection. Identifying the role you play in conversations and relationships allows you to set boundaries and avoid emotional overinvestment:

What is my role in this conversation?
Am I taking on more than necessary?

The circle back. This step reinforces trust by following up after initial conversations, showing care, concern, and faith in the other person's ability to progress on their own terms.

Strengths-based approach. Always highlight efforts and strengths, no matter how small, to build confidence and inspire progress.

Creating space for others and yourself. The goal is to empower others without absorbing their burdens, leading to more focused, present connections.

Quick Exercise to Build Self-Awareness

Check-in practice. After a conversation, set a reminder to check in with the person. Use open-ended questions like:

"You've been in my thoughts; any updates?"
"How are things going since we last talked?"
"Is there anything I can support you with?"

This exercise will help you nurture meaningful connections without solving other people's problems. Applying this mindset, you're not only assisting others but also preserving your own mental and emotional space. Each pause, every circle back, and each act of empathy redefines your role in relationships, establishing clearer boundaries and fostering authentic connections. This approach creates a ripple effect, building deeper trust, reducing the risk of burnout, and liberating you from the shackles of serial fixing.

Chapter 14

Redefining Empathetic Relationships

Whether warranted or not, I used to get a little self-conscious when introducing this framework to an audience. My Inner-Pleaser poked and prodded to ensure I didn't come off as unempathetic or dismissive. I worried that presenting a structure focused on boundaries might make me seem detached or overly rigid, and I was hyperaware of how people might interpret my words. This internal dialogue would constantly run through my head: What if they think I don't care enough? What if they misinterpret my intentions? But over time, I realized that these fears were rooted in my own discomfort with boundaries, not in the framework itself.

The "Support, Don't Solve" model is not about withholding care or compassion—it's the opposite. It's about creating an environment where empathy and empowerment coexist. Empathy isn't just about feeling for someone but about being present without taking over and about giving others the space to solve their own problems. I learned that when I introduce healthy boundaries, I actually give others more respect and trust, not less. Boundaries allow us to continue offering support without losing ourselves in the process, preventing burnout and compassion fatigue, which only make us less effective in helping others.

This self-awareness helped me redefine what it meant to show up fully for someone. I started to trust the framework more deeply, understanding that true empathy comes with the wisdom to know when to step back and when to engage. I became more confident in delivering this approach, recognizing that the power of the framework lies in its ability to foster deeper, more sustainable connections without draining the energy of either party. Over time, I realized that not only was this framework transforming my own life, but it was also resonating deeply with others. Those I introduced it to found themselves empowered, less overwhelmed, and more connected in their relationships.

When we resist the urge to immediately solve someone's problem and instead focus on empowering them, we cultivate long-lasting resilience and autonomy. This approach doesn't make us less compassionate—it makes us more effective leaders, friends, and supporters. It provides us with the tools to be present in ways that truly matter, without sacrificing our own well-being.

Caregivers in any form understand the precious bond and opportunity that presents itself when you pay attention and prioritize someone's needs or feelings. Comprehending the emotions of others and their needs even in times when words are not used is one of the purest forms of human connection. Neglecting to create space for ourselves even while we're opening ourselves to the emotions of others takes away from the beauty of our care and can lead to exhaustion, codependency, and resentment.

Becoming a space creator and subscribing to a "Support, Don't Solve" mentality provides that healthy balance between embracing your ability to decode and empathize on the one hand, while on the other hand incorporating the boundaries necessary for others to flourish and get their reps in. It authentically confirms your commitment to others and their situations rather than using them as platforms to compare, stroke your ego, or distract from your own issues.

When you fully embrace the "Support, Don't Solve" model, your stress, anger, and confusion will decrease because you'll stop taking false ownership of someone else's hurdle. Your need to control and fixate on others' agendas or lack of progress will dwindle. It is not that you don't care, you just have embraced a new role. One that is more balanced and honors the concept that everyone is in different places, carries different pasts, and is influenced by different worries and emotions. As you develop as a space creator, you will notice that your efforts and ability to create space for others actually provide you with the opportunity to create more space for yourself. Your mind will declutter, and you'll find it much easier to maintain presence.

You have the ability to foster this change within yourself, creating meaningful relationships and a greater sense of peace. You'll start to notice how these shifts in perspective and behavior lead to stronger, more authentic connections with others.

In your quest to become a space creator, you'll discover the transformative power of adaptability and resilience. Life is full of unpredictable moments and uncertainty, but your ability to respond with empathy without taking false ownership will allow you to continue to nurture without falling victim to compassion fatigue and burnout. The goal is not to fix or solve. Respecting others' processes, even if they are drastically different from your own, requires patience, intelligence, and confidence in your ability to connect and support others. This, like anything, takes reps and deliberation. This is not only a commitment to those you interact with, but to yourself. The key is attaining clarity of your roles and believing that in order to successfully fulfill those roles, you must maintain and nurture the relationship you have with yourself. Don't lose your vibrant passion for serving, helping, and guiding those around you. You can help others while preserving yourself and your boundaries.

As I began writing this book, I kept receiving familiar advice—something I've heard since I was young: "Zero in, Leah. What's your main goal? What's your overarching passion? Who is your target audience?" These questions were intended to guide me toward focusing, narrowing in on one thing. The concept makes sense, especially given that so many studies show that homing in on a single goal leads to mastery. I've never fully subscribed to that idea, and in many ways, not fully subscribing to this idea has served me well. I was the kid who had to try everything, eager to be part of it all—even at the cost of burning out. Over time, I've learned to balance my relentless curiosity and drive to experience it all with the non-negotiable roles in my life, like being a parent.

At first, I wasn't entirely sure who my exact target audience was for this book. Even now, I'm still not completely certain. But as I reach the book's conclusion, I can confidently say, "It doesn't matter." This book is for anyone who seeks connection, values relationships, and prioritizes others' well-being, yet struggles to balance those priorities with anxiety-driven motivations and the challenge of offering themselves the same care and attention they give others.

One of my hopes is that, through reading this book, you've learned something meaningful about yourself. While I provide a framework you can follow, the real takeaway is knowing how to implement the self-care and leadership tactics that we've all been introduced to but may not have applied consistently. Experts, teachers, clinicians, parents, and leaders have all shared tools for success, even if we haven't always put them to use.

As you continue on the path to becoming a recovering serial fixer (you'll get there with reps), you'll create more space to apply those valuable lessons. More importantly, you'll start to understand the internal resistance you may have faced along the way. We are all capable of change, but true lasting change occurs when we take the time to dig beneath the surface, resisting the gravity of quick fixes, temporary solutions, and the need to derive our sense of purpose solely from solving other people's problems. Before the book concludes, let's revisit the scenario from the beginning and replay what that day would look like if boundaries were intact and self-care was viewed as a nonnegotiable.

5:30 a.m.: Your alarm goes off, and you take a moment to breathe deeply. The warmth of your bed tempts you to stay, but you remind yourself how much better your day flows when you start it with some stretching. Committed to prioritizing your well-being, you swing your legs out of bed and begin, inviting the morning air in to clear your mind. Your brother's cryptic text from last night briefly crosses your thoughts, but instead of letting it linger, you remind yourself that you've done what you can for now and will follow up after your morning routine.

6:30 a.m.: After your short stretching routine, you grab your phone for the first time. A text from your neighbor asks for help with the school run. You pause before replying, carefully assessing your day. It's full but manageable—if you don't overcommit. You gently decline, offering a suggestion for a carpool schedule that might work better in the future. As you pour your coffee, a wave of relief washes over you. You've honored your limits, and it feels good.

8:00 a.m.: Your phone buzzes with a coworker's request for help. This time, you ask her to clarify her needs and set a boundary. "I can certainly help review your draft after lunch, but I've only got twenty minutes." You hit send and feel a quiet sense of pride. You've supported her without taking on more than you can handle, sidestepping the urge to "fix" everything like you habitually did before.

12:30 p.m.: Lunchtime is sacred and serves as a midday reset. You step outside for a quick walk, savoring the fresh air as you enjoy your sandwich away from your desk. Instead of scrolling through social media, you take a moment to mentally check in with yourself. After a quick chat with a nearby colleague, you begin preparing for the second half of your day, feeling more grounded.

3:00 p.m.: Your brother texts again, opening up about his struggles. You take a deep breath and call him. You hear yourself say, "I can understand how this is really taking a toll on you. I'm here to listen, but I think this might be bigger than what I can help with. I want to support you in finding the right kind of help for this." Letting go of the need to solve his problem isn't easy, but you've learned that true support often means encouraging others to seek the help they need while still being there in ways you can.

5:00 p.m.: The workday winds down, and you finish with time to spare to catch up on a few emails. Your coworker thanks you for your thoughtful feedback on her project, and you feel a sense of accomplishment—not because you fixed her problem, but because you empowered her to succeed with suggestions and not assuming the work yourself.

7:30 p.m.: Evening settles in with a well-earned sense of calm. Dinner is finished, and the family cleanup is complete—teamwork in action! Carpool duties are behind you, and now, it's time to relax. Your InnerCritic nudges you with whispers of unfinished tasks, but you've learned how to manage this voice. Gently, you remind yourself that tomorrow is another day, trusting that everything will be accomplished in due time.

Your teenager joins you, sharing frustrations about school. You listen attentively, resisting the impulse to jump in with solutions. Instead, you validate her feelings: "That sounds like a lot. I can see how hard you're trying. What's your next step?" Her face softens, and she begins to open up even more.

Later, you scroll through social media, but remain mindful of the boundaries you've set. You carve out time just for yourself—sipping something warm and cuddling with your dog. Instead of overstimulating or filling the quiet, you embrace the stillness, allowing it to prepare you for a restful night's sleep.

You've grown better at being present. As you reflect, you realize how much more fulfilled you feel, having balanced compassion for others with compassion for yourself. As the day ends, a profound truth settles in: Doing less doesn't mean you care less. It means you've chosen to show up with intention, preserving the energy and relationships that truly matter.

To all of you who've long felt the need to jump in and fix, I invite you to take what you've learned and start small. Begin by noticing when you're slipping into problem-solving mode. Instead, pause—offer support, create space, and observe what unfolds. You'll likely be surprised by the growth, both in yourself and in those you care for.

Ask yourself: As a serial fixer, how will I begin creating space—for others and for myself—today?

Acknowledgments

To my clients, whose courage and vulnerability have been some of my greatest teachers—thank you for shaping this work in ways beyond measure.

To my husband, for your loving encouragement and sharp editorial eye. To my beautiful daughters, thank you for your patience and understanding throughout the writing process.

To my parents and my sister, your love and belief in me have always been my foundation. Thank you for being my greatest cheerleaders throughout every stage of life.

To my friends, thank you for your motivating check-ins and for keeping me grounded. To all of my coaches and teammates along the way, who taught me to stay both humble and hungry.

To my beta readers, thank you for your thoughtful feedback. To Broadleaf Books and Lisa Kloskin, my editor, for your guidance and for helping me refine this work, and to Amanda Bernardi, my agent, for believing in me and making this dream possible.

To the companies and organizations I've had the privilege of collaborating with over the years—thank you for your trust and for opening doors that provided invaluable reps.

And finally, to my InnerCritic—thank you for pushing me to take risks, give my all, and strive to be my best. Aligning with you has given me an invaluable, present-day teammate.